T0214914

Practical Biometrics

Julian Ashbourn

Practical Biometrics

From Aspiration to Implementation

Second Edition

Julian Ashbourn
Biometrics Research
Berkhamsted, Hertfordshire, UK

ISBN 978-1-4471-6822-5   ISBN 978-1-4471-6717-4   (eBook)
DOI 10.1007/978-1-4471-6717-4

Springer London Heidelberg New York Dordrecht

© Springer-Verlag London 2004, 2015
Softcover reprint of the hardcover 2nd edition 2015
This work is subject to copyright. All rights are reserved by the Publisher, whether the whole or part of the material is concerned, specifically the rights of translation, reprinting, reuse of illustrations, recitation, broadcasting, reproduction on microfilms or in any other physical way, and transmission or information storage and retrieval, electronic adaptation, computer software, or by similar or dissimilar methodology now known or hereafter developed.
The use of general descriptive names, registered names, trademarks, service marks, etc. in this publication does not imply, even in the absence of a specific statement, that such names are exempt from the relevant protective laws and regulations and therefore free for general use.
The publisher, the authors and the editors are safe to assume that the advice and information in this book are believed to be true and accurate at the date of publication. Neither the publisher nor the authors or the editors give a warranty, express or implied, with respect to the material contained herein or for any errors or omissions that may have been made.

Printed on acid-free paper

Springer-Verlag London Ltd. is part of Springer Science+Business Media (www.springer.com)

This book is dedicated to all those who have struggled to find practical and socially acceptable ways of implementing biometric identity verification techniques upon a large scale. It is further dedicated to all the users who will be exposed to the many variations of biometric identity verification in the coming years and their inevitable curiosity as to what is actually happening behind the scenes and why.

"Julian Ashbourn has done a masterful job of presenting a holistic approach for incorporating biometrics technologies into new or existing systems in "Practical Biometrics." A renowned authority within the global biometric community, Julian's perspectives inspire us to realize what "should be done" versus what "could be done." He brings foresight and ethics to the table of mathematicians, scientists, engineers, and application owners to challenge us to ensure positive societal impacts of the use of artificially intelligent technologies – in particular, biometrics. Using the "BANTAM" methodology, Julian informs how biometrics might be deployed in everyday situations. In accordance with the guidance given in "Practical Biometrics," application developers and product designers/developers will optimize successful biometrics integration. I encourage readers to consider Julian's guidance and look forward to his future insights and recommendations."

Cynthia Musselman, Musselman's Authentication SMEs.

Foreword

It is an honour and a pleasure to comment on this second edition of *Practical Biometrics*. Julian Ashbourn provided us in 2006 with a very helpful book, but after nearly a decade, a second edition is badly needed. This is partly due to changing technology, but also because of changing user needs and behaviour and evolving social factors and conditions. Although much has changed since the appearance of the first edition, the gap between what biometrics should contribute towards a safer society and its actual contribution has only been getting wider and deeper.

What hasn't changed, though, is the fact that biometrics is our one and only means of recognising people making use of a person's individual physical characteristics. Most current admission and security systems are based on the use of administrative data that are not physically linked to the person involved. Even in the security business, many people do not realise on a daily basis that we have no defence against what I call *the wrong person*: we only tend to check whether the data provided corresponds with a token, a user name and any other code or password in our system. We then unthinkingly assume the person to be the right one. Thus, biometrics are indispensable for a safe society.

But the concept of biometrics also confronts us with some confusing concepts that are difficult to change:

Firstly, in the context of biometrics we often use the concept of identity verification without realising that this precisely is what biometrics cannot do! Recognising people is not more than a precondition for establishing someone's identity based on other data and documents. In addition, between recognition and attributing an identity, there is spacious room for interpretation errors and manipulation. To be able to monitor interpretation errors and detect manipulation by the person involved, we need more insight into the technology and the practise of biometrics.

Secondly, we tend to forget that repeatedly measuring a specific physical characteristic of the same person inherently produces slightly different measurement results. So, a biometric recognition is based on a statistical evaluation of these differences when assessing the probability that the person is the right one. If we want more certainty, more than one physical characteristic or biometric technique should be used at the same time. This is only effective if these are independent of each other and cannot be manipulated in the same way at the same time. Thus, the practice of biometrics is far from easy to understand or to organise.

Thirdly, we mostly have small-scale models and theories in mind, while application of biometrics is inherently large scale, either by the size or the extent of the process to be secured or by unintended negative spill-over effects in other processes. Generally, this causes overestimating benefits and underestimating problems. In addition, biometrically secured large-scale systems tend to behave differently than we anticipate and might even produce reverse results which, depending on the application's scale, might go unnoticed for a long time. So, biometrics not only provides us with solutions, but causes existing problems to get bigger and new problems to arise, as well.

These considerations may convincingly explain why I am happy with this second edition of *Practical Biometrics*, updated to reflect current trends in technology and the use of biometrics. In the next edition, I would appreciate some attention to the legal restrictions on the use of biometric data, especially in international applications. The requirements and limits differ from one legal culture to another, thus causing big problems for the prevention of identity theft and identity fraud in these vital large-scale applications unless these are taken into account while designing the system.

Biometrics are badly needed in vital parts of our society, and more insight into the technology and practise is essential. But we cannot wait until our insight is up to our security requirements. We have to learn while doing. This is why Julian Ashbourn's book is so very useful, as it is written with this learning process in mind.

Jan Grijpink (1946) is an Emeritus Professor of Information Science at Utrecht University where he part-time lectured in Chain-computerisation from 2004 until his retirement in 2011.

He studied Economics (1969) and Law (1971) at Groningen University and Management Science (1976) in Utrecht (SIOO). In 1997 he obtained his doctorate at Eindhoven Technical University with a thesis about Chain-computerisation. As Principal Adviser at the Dutch Ministry of Justice until his retirement in 2011, he focused on information strategy and identity issues.

From 2006 to 2012 he was Chairman of the Netherlands Biometrics Forum.

He is Senior Adviser of PBLQ, Center of Expertise, IT consultants of the Dutch government, The Hague.

He is Editor-in-Chief of the open-access Journal of Chain-computerisation (http://jcc.library.uu.nl).

Jan Grijpink regularly publishes on identity issues in a complex information society often using his special focus on large-scale information systems and chain-interdependencies to uncover hidden problems or develop better solutions.

Utrecht University   Jan Grijpink
The Hague, The Netherlands

Netherlands Biometrics Forum
The Hague, The Netherlands
March 22, 2015

Preface

Biometric verification techniques have been available for many years. Although the principle of using a biometric can be traced back to ancient times, the concept of commercially available devices with which to automate biometric identity verification was effectively a product of the late 1960s, with further development through the 1970s and 1980s leading to a step up in interest in the late 1980s. By the early 1990s, there were a raft of biometric device manufacturers offering a range of techniques including hand geometry, retinal scanning, fingerprints, voice verification, signature verification, and facial recognition. These were soon to be complemented by iris recognition, finger geometry, vein recognition, and other techniques, providing an intriguing technology choice for early adopters.

In parallel with technological development, we witnessed a good deal of investment in what was considered to be a technology on the brink of massive adoption across a broad scale of applications. The beginning of each year in the 1990s was marked with optimism that this would be the year for biometrics. The end of each year was marked with confusion and puzzled expressions on the faces of those who confidently predicted an explosion in growth for the industry. It simply never happened in the way the predictions suggested. Instead we saw a steadily but slowly increasing trickle of adoption in specific application areas, often in military or government/public service scenarios. These included applications in prisons, schools and universities, and at airports, primarily for access control purposes. We should be grateful to these early adopters, even with regard to applications which subsequently failed and were withdrawn, because they provided an opportunity to learn about the practical implementation of the technology, together with some of the technical and nontechnical issues highlighted as a result. Whether we have learned all of these lessons is rather debatable as many consultants and practitioners still rely on theoretical device performance metrics as the basis for developing related solutions. Those who have been close to the technology and its potential applications from the beginning know that there is a little more to it than this, especially when we are considering large-scale applications in the public domain.

Against the background depicted above, there have been many tackling the issues which they perceived as hurdles to wider-scale adoption. These included factors such as best practice in testing, API standards for interfacing to devices, and general interoperability. A great deal of good work has been undertaken in these areas, much of it on a voluntary basis, and this has served to create a more sustainable platform for future development. However, while we have pushed forward the understanding and articulation of many of the technical issues, there still exists a raft of other issues to consider around human factors, environment, and general infrastructure, which are especially pertinent to wider-scale adoption. This book will explore many such issues.

The concept of biometric identity verification may have progressed at a more natural pace had it not been for the tragic events in September 2001 which brought with them a renewed focus on identity verification in general. Ideas which had been simmering in the background were suddenly brought forward. Funding which had hitherto proved elusive was suddenly within reach. It was natural to explore related technologies and ascertain their potential for wider adoption. The concept of biometric identity verification was now in the forefront of such thinking. Since that time, and amid a changing political world background, biometrics have been increasingly used in a military context and, sometimes, for less than obvious applications. More recently, the explosion in the use of mobile devices has brought a new focus to the potential use of biometrics to help secure access both to the device in question and to transactions undertaken via the device. This development will expand the usage of biometrics dramatically and, no doubt, be instrumental in developing a culture change toward biometrics and identity management in general.

If we are to implement the myriad of suggested applications in a workable, sustainable, and socially acceptable manner, then we must understand the real implications of using this technology upon a wide scale, not for tens or hundreds of users, but for tens of millions of users, not only in carefully controlled operational environments where time is of no consequence, but in everyday public situations where timing can be critical. In addition, there are a plethora of background processes which need to be examined, from managing data through to training related personnel. This book, together with companion titles from the same author, published by Springer, will serve as practical hands on guides to make biometric technology work in real-life scenarios.

March 2015   Julian Ashbourn

Acknowledgement

Very special thanks to all at Springer-Verlag London Ltd, for their enduring support throughout the creation of this book and others in the series.

Contents

Introduction

1

This is the second edition of a book about biometrics and the deployment of biometric identity verification techniques in relation to operational systems in both the private and public sector. Such developments often arouse controversy because of the intensely personal nature of biometrics and their alignment with personal identity. Are we moving towards a big brother world to the detriment of all citizens? Can large organisations and governments be trusted to manage such personal data in a competent and ethical manner? Will the introduction of such techniques in relation to wide-scale public applications turn out to be a blessing or a curse? Is the technology really as foolproof as some vendors would have us believe? Such questions and concerns must be properly taken into consideration of course, but some will argue that it is not so much the technology we must beware of but the manner in which it is implemented. In order to design and implement any application properly, we must understand all of the associated issues. This has not been easy in the field of biometrics as there are many variables, some of which have little to do with the technology itself but nevertheless influence operational performance. This book will therefore take a fresh look at what it takes to integrate biometrics into wider applications. It updates the first edition with revised information and two new sections which serve to provide a more complete coverage of the subject and a better understanding of the broader scenario. But first, let us backtrack a little.

In contemporary terms a biometrics is perhaps best described as a physiological or behavioural trait which may be measured, recorded and subsequently compared to another sample in order to confirm an individual's claimed identity. The principle is not new and has been practised since ancient times, although in modern terms we equate biometrics with the automatic measurement and subsequent recognition of such traits via electronic devices. In this context, we may think of modern biometrics as a technology with its roots in the late 1960s, although it took a decade or two to resolve into workable operation. For further information about the history and development of biometrics, the reader may like to refer to *Biometrics: Advanced Identity Verification*, also published by Springer, ISBN 1-85233-243-3.

© Springer-Verlag London 2015
J. Ashbourn, *Practical Biometrics*, DOI 10.1007/978-1-4471-6717-4_1

The principles of operation with regard to contemporary biometrics may be generalised as follows. The biometric trait is captured via a suitable capture device, usually during a registration process at which other information about the individual in question is also gathered. (It is also possible to capture the biometric trait covertly, via a camera or hidden sensor, e.g. although the applications for such an approach may be highly questionable from both an ethical and practical perspective. Nevertheless, we shall witness an increasing use of this approach.) The captured biometric trait is typically converted into a reference template, which may be considered as the electronic representation of the trait. Ideally, this template should be derived in such a manner that it may not be reverse engineered to expose an image of the trait in question. However, more recently a direct image of the biometric trait has come to be considered as a reference template for many applications, even though this raises additional concerns around data storage and privacy. Within a conventional registration process, the reference template, together with other information as applicable, is typically stored as a record for the individual in question. Subsequent matching against this record is undertaken in two fundamentally different ways, verification and identification. Upon a verification or 'one-to-one' transaction, the user effectively claims an identity by providing some information such as a reference number, name or password which is typically used to call up a reference template from a database, in order that the user may supply a live biometrics to compare against this reference. An alternative verification method is for the user to supply the reference template from a portable token such as a chip card, identity card or mobile device, for example, and then provide a live biometrics to match against this reference. If the two templates match, according to defined criteria, then the user's identity is considered verified. Matching is a relative term however as the two templates will almost never match precisely, for a number of reasons including variability of live capture. The degree of required similarity in order to be considered as a match may often be programmed into the system as either a fixed or adjustable threshold ratio. Conversely, an identification or 'one-to-many' transaction is undertaken without the user having to supply any information other than their live biometrics. In this instance the live biometric data is compared against a database of reference templates and the user's identity determined as a match against one of these templates or, in some cases, several templates, requiring further analysis as appropriate. In this context, much depends upon the chosen biometric technique. A similar process may be undertaken remotely without the user being present, by comparing a single reference template against a database in order to find a match. Similarly, depending upon the chosen technique and the matching criteria employed, several potential matches may be returned via such a process.

There are various biometric techniques as well as variations within those techniques. Not all biometric techniques are widely used however and the currently popular examples may be summarised as follows:

- Fingerprints. The fingerprint is scanned electronically and a reference template created accordingly. This template may be derived from either minutiae elements, the pattern of the fingerprint or simply the image of the fingerprint.

Furthermore, the scanning, or capture process, may be undertaken upon the visible layer of the skin or, preferably, from just beneath the visible layer, the latter approach tending to be rather more reliable in practice as it is not influenced by minor surface abrasions. There are performance, interoperability and storage implications associated with the different fingerprint techniques.

- Hand geometry. A three-dimensional image of the hand is analysed and a template derived from this analysis. The hand geometry template (in the case of the industry-leading device) is typically small in size facilitating easy storage and transmission across a network.
- Iris recognition. The iris is captured via an infrared imaging process which distinguishes the iris from the pupil and sclera portions of the eye. A template is then derived from an analysis of the detail within the trabecula meshwork of the iris itself. This is typically undertaken by dividing the visible area into sections and analysing each section separately.
- Facial recognition. An image of the face is captured and analysed in order to derive a template. This analysis may take various forms, from plotting geometric points to greyscale analysis of pixels to determine boundaries, etc. Alternatively, an image of the face may simply be captured and used in a pattern-matching manner. There are also related variations such as thermal imaging techniques.
- Voice verification. The dynamics of vocal annunciation are partly a product of our vocal tract, mouth and nasal cavities and general physiological 'architecture'. The effects of these characteristics upon annunciation may effectively be captured by sampling the emitted sound and a representative template created for subsequent comparison with a live sample. Biometric voice verification should not be confused with speech recognition.
- Signature verification. The dynamics inherent in writing a signature may be captured along with the image of the signature itself, facilitating the creation of a representative template. The signature is of course a familiar identifier in many applications.

There are currently less widely used techniques such as vein checking, retinal scanning, ear lobe analysis, gait recognition, keyboard dynamics and scent which may continue to be developed for specific applications, and a steady interest into the possibilities of using DNA in this context continues, although DNA sampling is currently a complex process which is not instantaneous. There is also the concept of behavioural biometrics, including gesture biometrics in relation to mobile phones and even response biometrics which seeks to identify an individual according to responses to situations. However, some of these ideas are perhaps stretching the definition of biometrics as popularly understood a little too far. No doubt additional techniques will surface in time, but the list above serves our purpose for understanding what we mean by biometrics and indicating the variety of techniques which might be employed under this general banner. Occasionally, more than one technique is employed in relation to a given transaction, in what is typically referred to as multi-modal operation. Many border control applications employ just such a technique.

The question of which biometric technique is best is often asked. Of course, there is no overall 'best' biometrics. Different techniques have advantages and disadvantages depending upon the application and circumstances of its deployment. For example, in a physically dirty or abrasive environment, we would hesitate to deploy a contact technique such as fingerprints or hand geometry. Similarly, in an environment subject to strong variations in lighting and perhaps humidity, we may equally hesitate to deploy a technique which relies on cameras such as facial recognition. Similarly, an excessively noisy environment may not be particularly suitable for voice verification techniques and so on. We must also of course consider our user base and any special situations which might favour or preclude the use of a particular technique and also the relative operational performance requirements. So, as you can see, there is no best biometrics, only the most suitable biometric technique for a given situation. Helping to understand the variables and associated issues of such a situation is sometimes challenging, especially when we are considering wide-scale deployments.

Biometric identity verification has already been utilised in a wide variety of applications, some of which are outlined below.

- Prison systems. Within prisons, biometrics have been used for a variety of reasons, often connected with physical access control requirements for both staff and inmates. However, one of the more innovative and widespread applications has actually been for prison visitors. In many modern prisons dress is casual and, in communal meeting areas, it can be easy to confuse individual identity via visual cues alone, with obvious results. The application of biometric identity verification for prison visitors has been very effective in reducing this particular problem.
- Border control. There has been a fascination for using biometrics in relation to border control for more than two decades, with various trials being initiated and many systems remaining in place permanently. Techniques chosen have included hand geometry, fingerprints, iris recognition and facial recognition. Often the biometrics has either been contained on a token such as a chip card or referenced within a database via the reading of an associated token. An exception to this rule has been via the use of iris recognition using templates stored within a database and used in identification mode with no associated token. In recent years, biometrics are increasingly collected at the border point, irrespective of those contained on travel documents, allowing comprehensive databases to be built up and maintained within specific countries.
- Bank systems. Another idea that has fascinated for years and occasionally resulted in trial systems but rarely continued into the main stream, primarily for reasons of payback on implementation costs. Interestingly, in trials, users have often been very enthusiastic about the concept, especially where it has resulted in them receiving an additional level of service. Fingerprints and iris recognition have both been used successfully in conjunction with ATM machines in this context. However, this situation may soon change with the advent of mobile

payments wherein users will increasingly be offered the functionality of paying for low- and medium-value transactions via mobile devices.

- Voting systems. An interesting application where confidence as to the true identity of a voting individual can be as important as confidence that the same individual has not cast multiple votes. Various techniques have been tried including hand geometry and facial recognition, with interesting results. Much depends upon the robustness of the registration system of course.
- Entitlement systems. A good example of which has been on campus canteen systems, where only eligible students are able to claim subsidised meals, their biometrics being checked at access to the canteen. Similar deployments have been made for access to libraries and other campus facilities. Hand geometry has proved a popular technique in such applications, as have fingerprints.
- Computer and network access control. This has been possible for many years but it is only comparatively recently that reducing costs and simplicity of operation have made this a viable proposition for many organisations. Fingerprints lend themselves well to this application due to the small size of the readers and intuitive operation. Several notebook computers, tablet devices and computer peripherals are now available with integral fingerprint readers, and we shall undoubtedly see wider interest in this concept in the coming years, the concept being rejuvenated partly by mobile usage.
- Public services. We have already seen biometrics used in conjunction with health cards, benefit payment systems, drivers' licences, identity cards and other such applications. This is a trend which will undoubtedly continue, especially as public services are increasingly made available remotely where individual identity verification becomes particularly important.
- Payments will become an increasingly important application in the future as various entities move away from cash and, ultimately, even the use of traditional debit and credit cards. We are already seeing the first steps of such a culture change.

We could mention a number of other applications, some relatively mainstream and others more specific, but a glance at the above will provide an idea of the way people have been thinking about the deployment of this technology up until now. But what of future applications? Many of the applications mentioned above will be carried forwards into the future with refinements and variations as the technology continues to advance and people become more aware of how it may be used in these areas. In that respect, perhaps little has changed over the last decade where the progress of biometrics has been evolutionary rather than revolutionary. What has changed is the awakening of the government sector to the possibilities of using biometrics for wide-scale public applications such as identity cards, benefit systems and, following the events of 2001, travel. This is a very significant change from several perspectives and will undoubtedly accelerate the use of biometric identity verification in the public sector and see the initiation of various long-term projects. With the second edition of this book, we witness an increased public awareness around government aspirations in this context, as well as a different attitude towards technology in general and the use of biometrics in particular. Throughout the world we shall consequently see proposals which include ideas such as:

- The widespread implementation of national ID cards which include a biometric template on the card itself and maybe a corresponding template held on a central database.
- Entitlement cards, which perform an ID card role and additionally provide access to government or local services. Such a card might also be used to verify identity in relation to other commercial services. The biometric template may again be stored both on the card and on a central database, which may in turn be linked to other databases.
- Specific sector tokens such as health cards, drivers' licences, etc., which incorporate one or more biometrics. There are already many such cards in circulation in some countries, but we shall perhaps start to see extensions of this idea, undoubtedly with links to various associated databases.
- The almost ubiquitous use of passports which incorporate a biometrics. Such passports will incorporate one or more biometrics together with other information within an electronic chip, communicating via an RF link. They may be supplemented by biometric ID cards which may also be used for travel purposes.
- Wider-scale commercial applications such as banking, mobile commerce and online personal identity verification, which may use specific methodologies and associated tokens or perhaps take advantage of government-issued tokens.
- An explosion in the use of biometrics with mobile devices, including all manner of smartphones and tablets, in support of both general security and payments.

Depending upon your point of view, you may see the above as potentially exciting developments or potential disasters, especially with regard to individual privacy and the confidentiality of data. The issue here is not so much the use of a biometrics but how the back-end data is coordinated and what decisions are made as a result of checking against this data. Here lies the challenge of implementing wide-scale public systems which seek to use biometrics to bind individuals to identities and data histories. In some countries, there is little confidence in the ability of government to initiate and run large-scale IT systems in a secure and ethical manner. This seems to especially be the case where such systems are partly or wholly outsourced to commercial entities. Adding biometric identity verification for citizens to this scenario without a great deal of planning and subsequent control could have negative effects, both on the operation of the system at hand and also on the levels of trust between government and citizens. This is a very serious issue which requires equally serious consideration if we are to make the transition to large-scale systems in a practical and sustainable manner. There are many assumptions being made in this context which, ultimately, will prove to be incorrect.

So what of the future? Samuel Johnson (1709–1784) wrote 'Tomorrow is an old deceiver, and his cheat never grows stale'. We might do well to remember these words when we are visualising the benefits of a brave new world where citizens are biometrically checked in relation to just about any transaction or interaction with the state or commercial institutions. We might also do well to revaluate the purpose and role of the state in relation to citizens and their affairs. There have been some interesting observations made in this context over the years. For example, US novelist E.L. Doctorow wrote 'In the twentieth century ... governments have become very intimate with people, most always to their detriment'. While Emma Goldman (1868–1940) wrote 'The State is the altar of political freedom and, like the religious altar, it is maintained for the purpose of human sacrifice'. On a more positive note journalist Walter Lippmann (1889–1974) observed 'in a free society the state does not administer the affairs of men. It administers justice among men who conduct their own affairs'. Whatever your private view of the relationship between individual and state, there is no doubt that the trend in recent years has been for the state to hold more and more information about the individual and to share that information with other agencies when and where it thinks it appropriate to do so. Most recently, this situation has become accentuated under the banner of 'national and international security' and we shall undoubtedly see an increasing ability of the state to track the individual and maintain audit trails to build a individual profile which, in turn, may be used in decision-making processes for the provision of government or other services or maybe in the pursuance of legal proceedings. When we introduce a biometrics into the equation, we are more effectively binding an individual to this audit trail and relating profile. This may encourage a stronger level of confidence as to associated decisions made upon this data. At first glance, this may all appear fine, providing that the data is correct to start with and that the individual bound to it is really who we think. Unfortunately, this will not always be the case. We shall discuss such points elsewhere in the book.

In the future then, we shall start to see a requirement to give our biometric data in relation to a number of activities, from cross-border travel to interfacing with local and regional government, to everyday payment transactions. This situation will inevitably be reflected in the private sector as people become familiar with the concept and will perhaps be required to verify their identity in this way at the bank, supermarket, and club, online and in a variety of other everyday situations. Future generations will grow up with an acceptance of using their fingerprints, iris or other biometric trait in relation to everyday transactions as the norm and to expect personal profiles to be held on national databases. They may also use a biometrics to access everyday technological services and devices such as mobile phones, televisions and computers. They may use a similar technique to pass through a barrier at the railway station, to enter their educational centre or attend a theatre, being automatically billed in the process. If this is the future we are building, then we should endeavour to build it in a robust and fair manner which delivers tangible benefit while minimising further erosion of individual privacy. The introduction of such a fundamental societal change requires our very best efforts in order to fully understand the implications and mechanisms of implementation. Currently, this understanding is distorted (some would say deliberately so) in order to support agendas in both politics and commerce. We should beware of such distortions as they will lead to implementations which are not in the interest of the common good.

1.1   Why This Book Exists

As we might surmise from the above, the world is changing and it is changing fast. The last decade alone has seen the introduction of ideas and technology, as well as societal trends, that our grandparents would probably have not believed had it been suggested to them. We might loosely categorise these changes into two groups. Firstly societal and political changes and secondly, changes brought about by the development of technology.

In the first instance, we have seen a greater movement of individuals around the globe as people migrate for economic and other reasons. This, in turn, has had a dramatic and irreversible effect upon the culture of those countries most affected. In parallel, we have witnessed a changing relationship between the individual and the state, with the state exerting ever-increasing control in many countries. A similar situation exists between corporations and the individual as the concept of customer service has given way to one almost of the customer serving the corporation. Such fundamental changes alter the way in which individuals think about themselves, each other and their relationships with entities such as large corporations and government. In real terms, there is increasingly less personal freedom and increasingly less personal choice, in spite of propaganda to the contrary. In addition, in many countries, the increasing cost of living places more pressure on everyday living and emphasises the gap between the haves and have-nots. In most parts of the world, we have more wealthy people than we have ever had, but we also have greater numbers of people who feel increasingly disenfranchised or separated from the popular marketing image of modern man, hence the continual unrest that we are witnessing within our modern, technological world. This situation drives the burgeoning underground economy and ever-increasing crime figures within societies which would no doubt describe themselves as affluent. In fact, if looked at from a more human perspective, such societies might better be described as fast becoming intellectually destitute. But this is the modern world. A world where, as we are repeatedly told, the only constant seems to be change, and this change is not always for the better.

In the second group, we have technological developments which, we are often told, are mostly led by information technology. While not strictly true, there is no doubt that developments in information technology have enabled developments in other areas to progress at a faster pace than would perhaps have otherwise been possible. One effect of this has been the loss of a good deal of conventional skill-based employment and an increase in what we laughably call the 'service' sector, populated with largely unskilled and relatively poorly trained individuals. At the other end of the scale, we have a larger number of people qualifying from universities and colleges with educations which do not necessarily equip them to best deal with the requirements of the modern world although, fortunately, there are distinguished exceptions to this rule. These individuals (often referred to as knowledge workers) move into industry and government and become managers and shapers of the future, regardless of their true ability or aptitude in the area of their deployment. I mention these developments because they are significant from a societal and psychological perspective as human beings interact with each other in the modern world. The information technology evangelists have for years predicted paperless offices and digital societies which revolve around information. While arguments have raged back and forth, the digital reality has slowly crept up on us and we are now indeed faced with a society which relies heavily on information and the digital infrastructure required to manipulate it, very often upon a global scale.

You might ask what all this has to do with the practical deployment of biometrics and why we need a second edition of this book. After all, the other books in this series provide a solid grounding into biometrics and how they might be deployed in everyday situations. But in this fast-changing world, there have been global developments since those titles were first published, which have changed the outlook for biometrics somewhat, together with some of the potential applications. To complement those titles, we now need to take a fresh look at the implications of a wider-scale deployment of these principles in both public and private sector scenarios. Those seeking to introduce such techniques need to understand more about the human factors involved in deployment and those who are potential end users of the technology need to understand more about how the technology will be deployed and what it means to them as an individual. This book therefore reaches deeper into such areas, in some respects blazing new trails in the process. This book will also prove valuable to the casual observer or sociologist who is interested in the introduction of such technologies to mainstream societal applications and what this might mean for the future. *Practical Biometrics* may therefore be thought of partly as a practical guide to deployment and partly as a basis upon which to develop one's own thinking and conclusions around the introduction of a technological technique which will undoubtedly have far-reaching consequences from a societal perspective.

The introductory chapters of this book, which deal with technical, human and implementation factors, provide a solid background understanding which may then be exercised through the interactive chapters dealing with the BANTAM Program Manager and the educational software utilities. After working through these sections, the reader will have a better-than-average understanding of what it takes to deploy biometric identity verification technology as an integral part of larger applications. They will also have access to some useful tools to help them on their way, together with an understanding of how to use them. This will prove invaluable to those with aspirations in this direction, as one of the historical problems with introducing biometrics, even upon a small scale, has been around the understanding of the human factors involved and how these impact operation, coupled to issues of deployment which may not seem at all obvious at first sight. If these areas have proved problematical with regard to relatively small closed-loop systems, they will have an even greater impact as we turn our attention to the deployment of wide-scale systems in the public domain. While much has been written on the perceived or assumed efficacy of biometric identity verification in a general sense, there

remains relatively little in the way of practical literature on the subject and even
less in terms of educational tools to help those developing related applications.
This book therefore provides a valuable reference for those involved in implementing
related applications or who otherwise have an interest in this technology.

Before moving on to the working chapters of this book, I would like to stress the
importance of understanding the human factors involved in the deployment of
biometrics and the associated ethical responsibilities of those driving such deployments. If we are basing our aspirations on the desire to have a stronger confidence
level as to the true identity of an individual in relation to a transaction and we are
seeking to make (largely automated) decisions based upon this increased confidence,
then we have to pay particular attention to security and authenticity of enrolment
as well as to areas of associated data security, protection and individual privacy.
At present, we do not have suitably qualified infrastructures or adequate standards
to facilitate deployment on the scale anticipated in some quarters. By the time this
book is published, we shall have moved a little closer towards this ideal, but there
will still be much to understand from a societal perspective. Whether we introduce
a valuable enhancement to societal interaction or an odious burden and unnecessary
complication for citizens will depend upon our in-depth understanding of the issues
involved and the integrity with which we pursue our aspirations. This is particularly
pertinent to the government sector where the propensity to outsource grand schemes
and subsequently misunderstand the detail and ethics of implementation is unfortunately very real in almost every country. There is also a certain irreversibility to
many of these real-world implementations which we must take into consideration
for the longer term. In many cases it will help if we stand back and ask ourselves
why we are seeking to introduce such measures, precisely who will benefit from
such an introduction and how. If our answers align readily to the concept of common good and an associated and sustainable business case, then we might be able to
develop some very interesting and worthwhile applications. In any event, we should
look beyond the immediate promise of the technology towards a longer-term
societal perspective which acknowledges political and technical changes in our
fast-moving global civilisation but does so in a societally sympathetic manner rather
than with an emphasis on predation or confrontation. To accomplish this, we must
develop a good understanding of all the issues associated with wide-scale deployment,
including those of a human and social nature. This book offers a starting point
towards such an understanding.

Technical Factors

2

With any newly emerging technology, we must strive to understand and develop the technical factors in such a way as to be able to adequately describe and test performance, to be able to calibrate devices and components in order to deliver a specified performance and to be able to describe and measure variations in both equipment and operational environment. This is exacting work which occasionally becomes a little tedious and fuels all manner of discussion, useful or otherwise, among those who spend their lives immersed in such pursuits. However, to a certain degree it is important and necessary, especially if we are to achieve interoperability between disparate systems and a baseline of minimal standards for both technical operation and supporting processes. While the concept of biometric identity verification is not new and, even from the electronics perspective, has been around in a well-developed and operable form since the late 1980s, there remain inconsistencies in design, configuration and operation, even though standardisation has been achieved in certain areas.

The interesting point about biometrics in this context is that we have a brace of variables to contend with which are not a direct product of the technology but which nevertheless affect technical performance and operation. If we adopt a component view of systems technology and associated architectures, we can reduce each known component to an understood collection of variables and characteristics, building in an appropriate response to every known operational condition. In this case however we have a systems component, in the shape of a human being, which is jam-packed with all manner of variables, many of which are difficult to predict. We also have environmental variables which may be outside of our immediate control and which interact with the human variables to provide an even richer complexity of possible operational conditions. So, we must understand the technical factors certainly, but we must also understand the precise context of deployment in order to predict the operational consequences of these factors in context. Technical specifications alone will tell us relatively little about the implications of deploying biometric identity verification on a broad scale. We must also understand the human factors involved

© Springer-Verlag London 2015
J. Ashbourn, *Practical Biometrics*, DOI 10.1007/978-1-4471-6717-4_2

as well as the scale and nature of the proposed implementation. The following chapters of this book should serve to help the reader to develop a more coherent understanding of the broader operational picture.

2.1   Understanding Biometric Performance

There are a series of popular biometric performance metrics which have served us well over the last decade or so. These include false accepts, false rejects and failure to enrol. There are however additional ways of considering the operational performance of biometric identity verification techniques and associated components, and we shall be considering these. But first, let's take a look at the simple metrics which are most quoted in relation to biometric devices.

- False accepts (or false matches). The likelihood, expressed in percentage terms, that an impostor will be accepted by the system which believes that a presented live biometric matches the reference template for a claimed identity or, in the case of a system working in identification mode, matches one of the templates within the template database.
- False rejects (or false non-matches). The likelihood, expressed in percentage terms, that the correct individual will be rejected by the system which believes that the presented live biometric does not match the reference template for the claimed identity or, in the case of a system working in identification mode, does not match any of the templates stored in the template database.
- Equal error rate. A metric which is occasionally provided to indicate, in percentage terms, an error rate whereby the instances of false acceptance and false rejection are approximately equal. However, there are some caveats associated with such metrics as false acceptance in particular is difficult to predict and measure in real-world scenarios.
- Failure to enrol. A situation whereupon an individual is unable to enrol their biometrics in order to create a template of suitable quality for subsequent automated operation. This condition may be expressed in percentage terms in relation to a known user base after every user has undertaken the enrolment process. There may be a number of reasons for such a failure, some of them obvious, such as physical disability, and some less obvious where the biometric trait in question is simply less distinct than average. There is an additional user psychology factor to take into consideration in this respect.
- Transaction times. Usually quoted as a theoretical time taken to match the live template against a reference sample. This may be quoted as a one-to-one match or a one-to-many match when using a template database. In either event it will not necessarily represent the reality as there are so many other variables to take into consideration within the context of a real application.

Note that you will also come across the terms 'false match' and 'false non-match' which may be substituted for false accept and false reject, as well as other terms relating to failure to enrol. These performance parameters may often be fine-tuned according to an adjustable threshold setting which biases the matching algorithm towards a stronger likelihood of either false accepts or false rejects, the two parameters typically being directly related. For example, we may adjust the threshold in one direction which makes the system more tolerant of minor differences and hence easier to use. This may lessen the instances of false rejects but increase the possibility of false accepts. Conversely, we may tighten up the threshold in order to make false accepts less likely but at the same time increase the possibility of false rejects as users will now have to be far more consistent in providing their live biometric sample. This concept of a single matching threshold setting applied to a specific operational node, or even the whole system, represents a relatively crude approach to the management of performance. It is an approach that has been followed by almost all systems providers and has been a consistent weakness in the design and operation of biometric systems. However, in recent times, the author has conceived and developed an alternative approach named the Proximity Matching Method, which operates along altogether different principles, aligning each individual template with its own threshold settings in order to provide a comparison which is directly relevant to the quality of the original template. Instead of expecting every user transaction to reach the same matching threshold, regardless of user and template variables, the Proximity Matching Method simply requires that a match be within a certain variance of the original template quality. This is a far more realistic approach which results in less errors while simultaneously increasing the accuracy of the matching transaction. This, in turn, means that we may adopt a greater confidence in the efficacy of the biometric matching process, regardless of the biometric technique employed. As such, it is a significant step forwards in biometric technology.

The failure to enrol parameter may also be affected by systems settings. Indeed, we may consciously configure the enrolment equipment and associated process in order to reject enrolments which do not produce a template of sufficient quality to be considered reliable in subsequent use. In many cases, the individual concerned may simply re-enrol in a more disciplined manner in order to be accepted by the system. In some cases, through no fault of their own, the individual may simply not be able to enrol to the required standard with that particular biometric trait. Obviously, the larger the user population being envisaged for a particular application, the more this will become an issue, and we shall have to carefully consider the fallback process accordingly. In many cases it will be possible for the individual to register and enrol a different biometric. Many systems now recognise multiple biometrics and would be able to cope with such a variance. However, the reasons for failure to enrol should be understood and captured for further reference. One might almost propose that a legitimate failure to enrol is itself a form of biometric.

The transaction time metric is a particularly questionable performance figure as it is nearly always quoted out of context. The theoretical time taken to match one biometric template against another, or indeed match one template within a database of templates, bears little relation to typical live operational scenarios. There are many other user and environmental variables to take into consideration before one can realistically propose a representative transaction time. The previously released

Pentakis software utility provided a module to assist with the calculation of transaction times, taking the manufacturers' specified figure as a starting point. This is a much more realistic approach to understanding what transaction times might actually be in relation to a proposed application. There are many variables to take into account including overall systems performance which, itself, may well be variable on both a temporal and spatial basis. In terms of live automated systems, such as those used for border control purposes, for example, one should not assume that the automated system will realise a greater user throughput. In many cases, it will not and there are various reasons why this might be the case, many of them non-technical in nature.

While the parameters discussed above have been used for more than two decades to describe the performance of different biometric techniques and individual devices within a given technique, they have not proved adequate to describe the realised performance of biometric systems under operational conditions. This is not to say that such metrics are not useful—they are, but that they should be viewed in context. They offer a useful indication of how a particular device might perform under certain conditions and as tested by the device manufacturer. This brings us to the question of exactly how the manufacturer tested their particular device or software in order to arrive at these figures. Was a device set up under laboratory conditions and calibrated in order to provide the most impressive performance figures? Or are such quoted figures simply derived from an extrapolation of theoretical performance based around the mathematics of the matching algorithm? If real test conditions were created, how many users and how many transactions were involved in the tests? What was the profile of the user base from an age, gender and ethnicity perspective? How familiar were the users with the system? Were they the same laboratory technicians who had been developing the system? One could continue, but you get the picture. There are a number of ways of producing theoretical performance figures for a given biometric device and its associated software. Such specifications are of academic interest, but we should not expect them to be necessarily realised in practice. In some instances, they may actually be improved upon (within an intelligently implemented system), but mostly the opposite will be true as we deploy real systems into real operational environments with real users. To state it simply, real operational environments are not easily replicated in the laboratory where most performance testing of this type takes place. One of the primary differences is the user base and their particular perspective of the system at hand. Couple this to the variances in environmental conditions and we have a set of complex situations which are far removed from the typical laboratory set-up. Device manufacturers and systems designers would therefore do well to study realised performance within a variety of operational conditions in order to understand true performance characteristics in relation to their favoured metrics. This is starting to happen in some instances but is still relatively rare.

We may also consider that the popular metrics as presented may not be best suited to our needs and that we need to supplement these with additional information. The User Psychology software utility referenced elsewhere in this book adds another metric named 'average error rate' or AER in order to provide a simple figure for comparison when evaluating different scenarios. We shall cover this in greater depth later on. We shall also cover some of the other factors which directly affect realised performance of automated biometric identity verification checks. Indeed, there are a great many such factors which combine to render the biometric matching transaction a more complex undertaking than many might suppose. This reality often tends to be oversimplified when discussing or implementing biometric systems, leading to an unqualified confidence in the efficacy of the same.

2.2   Understanding End-to-End Performance

One of the interesting paradoxes which arises when deliberating the use of biometrics is that people tend to engage in sometimes quite animated discussion around the conventional metrics in relation to a given device. If you recorded and analysed such discussions, you would probably conclude that 90 % of the conversation is focused upon the biometric device and its theoretical performance. The irony is that the biometric device represents only a very small part of a typical system which employs biometric identity verification techniques. Some people speak of biometric systems as though they were entities in their own right, but there is actually no such thing as a biometric system and we would do well to acknowledge this truth right from the start. Biometric identity verification techniques may be incorporated into a larger system which itself has clear objectives and purposes of operation. Such a system may already exist or may be created from scratch but, in any event, the biometric identity check represents a component part of a larger transaction. It is the larger transaction which is the primary focus and for which we shall be most interested in realised performance under true operational conditions. Naturally, we shall not wish the biometric check to adversely impact the overall transaction time or otherwise affect the smooth operation of the transaction. For this reason we are interested in the performance of the biometric check itself, from a number of perspectives including accuracy, timing and ease of use. However, we should be equally interested in the greater systems performance and, in particular, how it has been designed from an information security perspective.

It follows then that there are various ways of looking at performance. If we break the system down into physical and logical components, we can analyse the performance of each component under typical operational conditions and try to optimise the performance of each component in order to create a harmonious and efficient whole. This is fine in theory and in many cases will provide a representative view. As systems become larger and more complex, however, the number of variables which may be outside of our immediate control also becomes greater. For example, if we are deploying the system over existing networks, there will be both the inherent network performance to consider, as well as the variables such as adverse loading at peak times and the possibility of individual component failure. The advent of cloud technology and virtual machines brings additional variables into the equation. Much of this can be understood and allowed for within good systems designs, but there is always the unexpected to consider. We can appreciate therefore that even from a purely technical perspective, the realised performance of a particular system is somewhat dependent upon the end-to-end process, which must necessarily include all components involved in the chain in relation to a given transaction. When we introduce an automated biometric identity check into this process chain, we introduce a brace of additional variables which will have a direct influence upon systems performance. Some of these variables are physical and environmental, while some of them are of a more psychological nature. In many cases, psychological variances can introduce physiological change which, in turn, can produce physical interaction changes. We shall consider this element in greater depth when we look at the human factors but suffice it to say that the combination of human and environmental factors can influence the performance of that part of the transaction significantly. These variances will often dwarf those that exist between different transducers of the same biometric technique or even those fundamental variances between techniques.

It is of course the transaction which we are especially interested in from a performance perspective. We may have several types of transaction within our overall application, which we can classify in terms of expected frequency and overall importance. It may be that certain low-frequency, low-priority transactions can bear the load of slower realised performance. Conversely, high-priority access-related transactions may be required to be undertaken in real time with the absolute minimum of systems-induced delay. Picture, for example, an automated border control system where users are required to undertake a biometric check in conjunction with the production of a known document or token. Typically, we would wish the automated system to be at least as fast operationally as the manual equivalent. However, if the automated system is also required to perform additional tasks, such as referencing one or more external databases, compiling and logging the overall transaction and of course managing the biometric check and the related user interface, then we are cramming quite a lot of activity into a short time window. We also have to build exception handling into the equation as well as processes which allow users to make minor errors and recover from them within the course of normal transactions. Add on to this all the other systems-related, human factors and environmental variables, and the overall transaction time under typical operational conditions may be a little longer than anticipated. Note that it will certainly be quite different from the figure quoted by biometric device manufacturers and systems integrators.

Let us consider for a moment some of the items within the road map of a typical transaction of this type. Firstly, we must initiate the transaction, usually via a user-controlled event, such as presenting a token to the system (in our border control example, this might be, e.g. a chip card or smart passport). This token must be read by the system and certain information retrieved from it in order to identify the token together with salient information about the authorised holder of the token. Depending upon the precise nature of the application, the user may then be presented with options to pursue. It may be that we are already undertaking background checks on the information retrieved so far, by linking into other databases. The results of these checks may influence the options offered to the user. At a suitable point we shall prompt the user to provide their biometric sample for comparison against a reference biometric template. This reference template may be stored on the token presented by the user or may be held in a central database. In any event it shall need to be retrieved and made ready for comparison with the live sample. The live sample itself may or may not be of sufficient quality to make such a comparison practicable. For example, the biometric trait may have been poorly aligned (fingerprint, facial image, iris, etc.), necessitating a further attempt by the user in order to provide a suitable sample for comparison. At this point, the serviceability and calibration of the biometric capture device become pertinent. A dirty camera lens or slightly damaged fingerprint sensor will naturally have an effect, as will a poorly functioning token reader. Assuming everything is working perfectly, the biometric matching algorithm can be run and will return a result accordingly. If the result is positive and all the related checks have proved satisfactory, then the transaction can be compiled and logged (it may draw information from several sources), a suitable response displayed via the user interface and the user granted access, or the associated benefit, accordingly. Within this relatively simple example, there are many opportunities for delays to be introduced, either systems and network related or user related. The sum total of these transactional stages, plus the operational delays, will provide us with an overall end-to-end transaction time which, of course, will vary from transaction to transaction. We may derive a representative average transaction time once we have sufficient operational data to analyse. You may consider that small variances either way are not necessarily significant, but this will depend greatly upon the number of transactions via a given number of points of presence and what other processes these transactions feed into. In a busy international airport environment, for example, a difference of 3 or 4 s per transaction may prove to be quite significant. Similarly, in the context of an online transaction undertaken via a public network, a few seconds multiplied by a large number of users may prove significant. There are other scenarios of course, including those where a biometrics is captured covertly and matched against a database. In such instances, there may be other processes taking place which will influence the overall result of the transaction.

The concept of scalability springs to mind here. It is one thing to deploy a contained closed-loop application with a small number of constant and consistent users. It is quite another thing to deploy an application in the public domain with a potentially very large number of infrequent and sometimes inconsistent users. The scalability issues already understood from a systems component architectural perspective will be further compounded by the human and environmental factors. The concept of performance in this context must be viewed as end-to-end transactional performance under real operational conditions. In order to understand this concept, we must understand all of the variables involved and their potential impact upon the overall transaction. With regard to applications which incorporate a biometric identity check, there is a tendency to take the device manufacturer quoted transaction time figure and extrapolate this to the number of anticipated transactions at a given point of presence. Such an overly simplistic approach will however almost certainly provide you with the wrong answers upon which to base your application designs. It is essential to understand how the system will work under true operational conditions, what the variables might be and why and, especially, how these might influence overall performance. Thinking in terms of true end-to-end performance will help develop such an understanding. Please note that in the context of large-scale applications in the public domain, the development of such an understanding may require a considerable amount of research, especially where interaction with legacy systems is required. The infrastructural picture may become quite complex and this may require specialist skills in order to interpret the situation correctly and reach the right conclusions. The mushrooming of mobile technology and mobile networks introduces some interesting situations in this respect, as the infrastructure itself introduces additional variables. In addition, the systems security aspect of such infrastructures brings some additional factors to consider. Taking everything in this chapter into account will help you to understand the impact of introducing biometric identity verification into mainstream processes and what this means in terms of performance.

2.3 Designing Applications

It is perhaps pertinent to consider application development and how we might integrate biometric identity verification in a practical manner. Those responsible for application development will have a good understanding of contemporary IT architectures and associated methodologies to provide the functionality typically expected for applications within the corporate and governmental sphere. They will also have their favourite coding languages and development tools, with which they will be familiar, although this area is constantly changing, with a current emphasis on web services and portability across mobile and desktop clients. It is unlikely however that many mainstream application developers have experience of properly integrating biometrics into their applications and, although this isn't particularly difficult, it may be pertinent to discuss some of the fundamental areas for consideration in this respect.

The first of these areas should be a complete analysis of the application, its primary purpose and its inherent processes. For an existing application there will presumably be points at which some form of identity verification, perhaps via a password, already takes place, in which case there will almost certainly be some integration with directory services, possibly via the LDAP protocol. Is it appropriate to simply replace these instances with the biometric methodology, or should we take the opportunity to completely rethink and, if necessary, re-engineer the process? In many cases the latter will be true as the existing directory will probably not cater for the storage of reference biometric templates in its standard configuration. If we intend to store the biometric templates within the directory (which will typically be shared across the IT estate), then we must customise it for this purpose. If we intend to store the templates parochially within the application, then a suitable structure must be created which is both secure and of a suitable operational performance. Of course, we may not wish to store the biometrics at all but simply load it from an external token at the time of the identity verification transaction. This factor of where we store the reference biometrics is simply one of many which we shall need to take into consideration as we analyse the objectives and technical architecture of the application at hand. It follows then that we must fully understand the operational processes before we can best judge where and how the biometric identity check should be integrated. If we are starting with a clean sheet for a totally new application, then we must first fully understand the objectives of this application, in what environment it will be deployed, what the projected usage will be, how the security requirements relate to perceived risk, what assumptions are being made around the use of biometrics and so on. With a good understanding of the application's objectives and how it will be used, we may then turn our attention to the other fundamentals. However, before we leave this area, allow me to stress just how important an area it is. Without a robust and crystal clear understanding of these fundamental factors, all that follows is likely to be compromised in its functional efficiency and therefore the benefits provided. The BANTAM methodology provides for an efficient and complete way of mapping out these requirements at various levels, from high-level aspiration to low-level component design. It is highly recommended that you use this methodology right from the start with a new project, as a properly conceived and documented application development will pay dividends, not just throughout the development project life cycle but subsequently through ongoing maintenance, training and other areas. The standard BANTAM distribution is readily available online, as is the BANTAM Program Manager software, described elsewhere in this book. With the help of these tools, you are in a strong position to design and implement well-conceived and managed biometric programs.

The next area for our attention is the choice of biometric technique. There are many factors which may affect this choice, including human and environmental issues. Let's start with the operational environment. What are the characteristics of the environment where this application will be deployed? From the physical perspective, are we anticipating a protected internal environment? Is this environment regarded as 'clean' as in a typical office? Is the environment constant in terms of temperature, humidity and lighting? Is the environment noisy? We can readily appreciate that certain techniques are not suited to certain environments. For example, we would probably not choose to use optical fingerprint readers in an industrial workshop where the users' fingers are constantly contaminated with foreign matter. We may hesitate to use voice verification in a particularly noisy or acoustically volatile environment. We may not wish to employ cameras in an area of rapidly changing humidity or lighting conditions. Of course, the environment may not be fixed at all, or even known, if we are considering the use of biometrics with mobile devices, either for commercial, military or other usage. However, for now, we shall assume a fixed and known environment. While considering the physical environment, we would do well to also consider the electrical and data communications situation. What is the position with the main electricity supply to our proposed facility? This may be more variable than you think, both in rural and central areas. It is not just a question of continuity of supply but quality and consistency. Often, the national grid system involved will represent a constantly fluctuating balance of supply and demand wherein realised voltage might vary more than one supposes, especially at peak usage times. In addition, there may be a good deal of periodic electrical noise. If you are not using any form of mains filtering, you may like to revisit this area, and while you are at it, ask some questions about UPS policies. A key operational system should ideally have some form of uninterruptable power supply, unless this is unfeasible on a third-party site. With regard to data communications, are we anticipating the use of an existing network? Do we have any information about the performance of this network? Do we have statistics for bandwidth and capacity? Do we understand the current loading of this network and any variations according to peak-time usage? Do we understand if and how our proposed system will impact the network? Depending upon the chosen architecture, it may have a significant impact. Similar questions should be asked about data storage and disaster recovery policies. All of these areas and more should be carefully considered as part of the operational environment analysis. However, at this point we are especially concerned with developing a short list of biometric techniques which might be suitable for use within this particular environment. Of course, we may be thinking about an application spread across multiple environments, or within which multiple biometrics are used, in which case we shall have to understand all of them, together with the associated variables. All of this should be carefully researched and properly documented.

After arriving at our short list of possible biometric techniques, we may then usefully turn our attention to the user base and specific functionality envisaged. Analysis of our prospective user base may indicate that a certain proportion of users are likely to experience some operational difficulty with certain techniques. If this proportion is insignificant, we may choose to allow for it via exception handling routines and policies. If it is more significant, we shall have to consider the situation more carefully. The sort of factors which may influence this area could include age, gender, ethnicity and disability. If there are no perceived issues in this respect, we may like to consider the more psychological human factors. For example, do users have an inherent preference for one technology over another? Are there any objections to the use of a specific technology for cultural or personal reasons? These sorts of questions can often be addressed via timely and honest communication. If biometric identity verification is being introduced into a process for the first time, it would be worthwhile to involve prospective users with the project at the earliest possible time, ensuring that their views are taken into account and that any questions or concerns may be properly addressed. In many cases there will be no significant issues. However, if there are issues, you do not want to discover them at the time of implementation, at which point they may be doubly difficult to address. In this context, the Biometrics Constitution and Biometrics Charter documents, which are readily available from the Biometric Research website, will prove invaluable in helping to ask the right questions and documenting the overall proposal.

So, after properly considering the required functionality, the operational processes, the operational environment, the user-base profile and the anticipated usage, we are now in a position to choose an appropriate biometric technique in which we have confidence for our purpose. It is likely that we shall have a choice of product offerings, all no doubt suggesting excellent operation in our application. We shall have to make a choice as to our preferred devices and supporting software. Currently, there is little true interoperability in this respect, although this situation continues to improve. The developer may take advantage of common utilities such as the BioAPI, depending upon the level of application development being undertaken in house. We may also like to consider the architectural requirements at this point, especially with regard to biometric template storage. If the reference biometric template is to be stored only on a portable token, such as a chip card, then we have to consider how this data will be retrieved from the token and processed (or whether it is actually processed on the token, as will increasingly be the case with mobile devices). A primary question here will be where the matching process takes place, either within the biometric capture device itself or within the host software. In the latter instance, we shall have to consider data security and integrity as the data passes back and forth, as well as protection against the likelihood of an attack by interfering with this process (i.e. injecting a 'passed' result into the system). If we plan to store the biometric reference templates in a central database or directory, then we must additionally consider where this database sits and how it will be accessed. If we plan on using replicated or distributed databases, then there will be additional data security and integrity issues to address for this model. Depending upon the technology chosen and other on-site systems, it may be that the biometric devices are connected to remote processors or network nodes. If this is the case, then the precise functionality and operational methodology of these devices need to be understood and incorporated in the broader architecture. One should consider the entire end-to-end process and the data flow throughout this process, noting where relevant data is stored and how it is referenced. If a PKI (public key infrastructure) is involved, then this too must be understood in detail and absorbed into the overall design. This broader architectural perspective may be defined and properly documented using the BANTAM methodology. This, in turn, will render application design and development a good deal easier as the underlying architecture will have been defined in advance.

Having resolved the above, we may now turn our attention to application development proper. Assuming the core functionality of our application is understood, we shall focus on the integration of the biometric identity check. There are several approaches to this issue, depending upon the precise functionality required (if we are simply providing network access control, e.g. we shall probably find some suitable software available directly from the device vendor). Assuming some specific functionality is sought, we shall need to integrate the biometric element into the main application. Many vendors provide software development kits (SDKs) to help us with this task. These typically comprise one or more DLLs (dynamic link libraries) or an API (application programming interface) plus the relevant documentation to describe the purpose of each DLL or API call. This sounds straightforward enough, but there may be issues to consider. Firstly, is this SDK compatible with the application development language and tools being used for this project? It is generally considered that DLLs written in C++ may be accessed from within most development environments, but this can sometimes be messy due to slightly differing data types, which may prevent the DLL calls from running, or worse, return subtle errors which are hard to identify. Assuming that the SDK is 100 % compatible with the development environment being used, we still need to ascertain the robustness of the associated DLLs and fully understand the various function calls. If an API is being used to access an existing application in a particular manner, perhaps via scripts running in the host application, then the process needs to be carefully tested in order to ensure reliable operation under all eventualities. We must similarly understand the procedures for trapping errors and what the error codes being returned really mean. The best approach here is thorough testing of the DLLs or API in a representative test environment, and adequate time should be allowed for this. We must also consider the user interface. Some SDKs may include ready-built dialogues for this purpose, but even when so supplied, you may wish to either customise or provide your own according to in-house policies of functionality and style. You will also need to consider how errors in the biometric-checking process relate to the core software and the associated process flow, together with the requirements for an audit trail. Of course, we shall also need to determine the exact points within the core application where the biometric identity check will be required and ensure that the user is prompted accordingly and that the appropriate devices are initiated in order to receive the live biometric. Most of this should be handled by the device manufacturer's DLLs, provided that the necessary drivers have been loaded on the host computer. Be aware that if using an SDK of any description which relies upon third-party DLLs or core applications, then the resulting application will have a dependency upon versioning. If the supplier introduces new versions of the core application or DLLs, then the entire application will need to be retested in order to ensure that existing functions operate reliably and that any new functionality operates as expected. This will always be an issue where third-party software code is utilised within the broader application, unless a decision is taken to freeze all such code and not to update to new versions. Beware also of dependencies upon intermediate-code run-times such as Java or dot Net and the versioning thereof. Similarly, if a proprietary third-party database is being used, there may well be a version dependency involved. While such issues are a product of the modern information technology world, many of them may effectively be removed via intelligent in-house design. In any event, they should be comprehensively documented and referenced as part of the overall maintenance and support plan for the application.

When we are satisfied as to the high-level interface with the biometric device, we may like to consider the wider architectural requirements, including the positioning of any biometric databases and how they are accessed, together with the relevant network protocols, etc. In this vein, we must also consider what set-up and configuration tools we need to supply to network administrators and support staff. These may include utilities to configure matching algorithm thresholds, or custom enrolment procedures, the management of digital certificates, and so on. We may also include custom diagnostic tools with which to analyse transaction results or query the biometric capture devices to check their calibration and operation from a centralised position. Naturally, any such utilities need to be vigorously tested and proven as to their own robustness and accuracy. Many, if not most, of these functions may be available via the SDK vendors, requiring little low-level coding on behalf of the application developer. This will represent a sensible approach in many instances. If, on the other hand, the application developer wishes to bypass available DLLs and develop their own low-level code, then they will need all the relevant information from the device manufacturer. This may not be easy in some instances, and, depending upon the scale and scope of the project, it may be that a joint venture between the technology supplier and application developer would represent a better approach. If the technology supplier supports the BioAPI common interface, then the application developer may like to acquaint themselves with this standard and ensure that their own code is compatible. This may prove beneficial in the longer term as it will allow for alternative biometric capture devices to be easily ported to the core application, should this be necessary. We must also consider audit trails and logging mechanisms. If the application is built upon a UNIX/Linux architecture, then we may take advantage of the inherent syslog functionality and route our transaction-specific information through this channel. The results may be analysed within a third-party log management tool or, alternatively, we may incorporate such functionality within our overall application design. This would be particularly pertinent if we are envisaging a centralised management function with a number of remote nodes communicating over a network.

The practical detail of integrating the biometric functionality with the core application will not prove troublesome to the competent application developer. What will require a little thinking through is the reality of operation and anticipating how the associated human factors and environmental conditions may affect realised performance in this respect. In particular, we should consider the equivalence of realised performance across operational nodes and what this means for both overall systems performance and systems configuration. This is a factor which has often been misunderstood and yet one which remains critically important if we are to have confidence in the overall operation of the application. This broader understanding will in turn enable us to build in to the core application software all the necessary exception handling routines and associated user feedback, which shall need to be integrated into an overall process flow. Defining and documenting this process flow will play a major part in the development of the core software. It is strongly recommended that you use the appropriate BANTAM maps for this task. This will facilitate discussion between all the relevant parties during the analysis phase and ensure that the application developer has the same understanding as the operational area responsible for implementing the application. Development houses will have their own ideas about software development methodologies and these may differ from organisation to organisation but will in any case include testing stages. One point to understand here is the difference between in-house testing and real deployments. In this respect it will be wise to conduct, in addition to interim testing of components, a thorough end-to-end test under real operational conditions before attempting to go live.

If you can involve real users in all these tests, then so much the better. If the application is going to be deployed over multiple sites, then of course a methodology must be devised to orchestrate this in a robust manner.

2.4   Understanding Interoperability

The term 'interoperability' can mean different things to different people depending upon where they are standing. To many, it will suggest interoperability at device level, enabling alternate devices to be substituted within a given application. This is one such definition certainly, and an important one. It has been in the minds of the biometric fraternity for many years, and as a result, we have seen the development of initiatives such as BioAPI, a common application programming interface for biometrics, and CBEFF, a common biometric exchange file format, and other initiatives aimed at interoperability. In the first instance (BioAPI), they facilitate a standard way of communicating with a biometric device from a software program-ming perspective. Thus, having written the necessary interface commands for device A, it should be possible to substitute device B, if they are of a compatible technique and both BioAPI compliant. In the second instance (CBEFF), they facilitate a common file format for passing biometric information between two entities, such as systems or components within a broader architecture. These are both useful developments and the teams responsible are to be congratulated on their achievement. To what extent these initiatives are embraced within more recent technological developments may be a little questionable, but they represent a good starting point for deliberations around interoperability.

However, when we are considering large-scale applications, particularly those in the public domain, then there are several other aspects of interoperability which we must consider. If we seek transactions across or between disparate systems, for example, then we must have, for each given technique, a common biometric tem-plate format. Let's imagine, for example, a fingerprint system which is operational across different government agencies in different geographic regions. I may have enrolled into system A in region 1 but be required also to undertake transactions via system B in region 2. To facilitate this, system B must be able to read my biometric template via its own equipment in a reliable manner which ensures that the biomet-ric identity matching process is equivalent. It must be able to do this even though I have never enrolled into system B. Similarly, individuals enrolled into system B must be able to be recognised via system A. For this to happen we need common biometric templates, as well as access to the reference templates across disparate systems. We might reasonably achieve this if all the equipment within both systems is identical and originates from the same supplier, but we cannot guarantee this. Therefore, we need a common template which can be read by disparate devices and systems. This has also occurred to the biometric fraternity and work has been under way for many years under the auspices of NIST (National Institute of Standards and Technology) and others, in order to arrive at template standards for the primary biometric techniques. This is a complex area which will require careful consideration if technical and operational compromises are to be avoided. The question of template quality is an interesting one to ponder in this context. We can prescribe certain aspects of this within a template standard (such as image quality, resolution, scaling, etc.), but how can we be certain that the captured biometric traits and the reference template created from them are of sufficient quality to be operationally reliable for the individual concerned, especially from the point of view of interoperability across disparate systems? Of course, we could simply assume that individuals will register into each system separately and provide their biometrics in order to create reference templates associated with each system (unless the reference is read into the system via a portable token). However, this would result in several templates for the same individual, each of which might be of a different quality and registered against slightly different demographic data. Furthermore, different systems will be configured differently with respect to the matching algorithms utilised and the threshold settings thereof, almost guaranteeing different levels of realised performance. In practice, we have a mixture of approaches where, very often, the reference biometrics is read into the host system from a token or document (such as a passport) and then the host system retains a copy of the biometrics for its own purposes. This situation raises additional questions around privacy and the security of data. Questions which are currently difficult to resolve as individual countries have different laws and attitudes in this respect.

This brings into focus another key area, the registration process. This in itself has different facets. Firstly, there is the technical efficiency and quality of the process, which determines the ultimate quality of the reference biometric template. Good-quality templates are essential for reliable subsequent operation. It follows then that we should define this technical process in some detail in order to be sure that we are creating reference templates of a consistent quality, even in different locations. Part of this definition should relate to the process itself (which in turn should be translated into a training programme for operators) and part to the specification and calibration of the biometric capture devices. Furthermore, the operational environment should be precisely defined in terms of lighting, temperature and humidity. We might also specify a minimum standard for supporting technology such as computers and computer monitors (which should be carefully calibrated). With the majority of biometric techniques, it will be possible to derive a quality rating for each created template, thus offering the possibility to reject a template which falls below a certain quality threshold and re-enrol the user accordingly. If this is possible with the technology chosen for a particular application, then a suitable quality threshold level should be decided upon and established as part of the registration process, being communicated to all registration stations accordingly. The other pertinent factor of the registration process is the authentication of the claimed identity via a series of background checks in association with documentary and other evidence provided by the enrollee. Clearly, we do not wish to legitimise a fraudulent identity by binding such an identity to a biometric template. We must therefore have confidence that our registration process is robust and unlikely to be compromised by fraudsters. This is a vitally important point. If individuals enrol into disparate applications under different identities (and possibly with different biometric traits), then we shall be effectively aiding and abetting the criminal world by conferring false identities upon individuals. This would be particularly unfortunate if the registration authorities were government agencies. There is no doubt whatsoever that this has already occurred on an alarming scale, with some countries (including those in the west) being notoriously lax in their standards and enthusiasm towards this primary identity verification. We may readily appreciate therefore that our process for checking the claimed identity prior to biometric registration must be as close to foolproof as we can render it. For an application which crosses boundaries of either department, organisation or possibly national borders, we must have an equal confidence in the registration process, wherever it is undertaken. Without this, true interoperability will never be realised and our confidence in the respective systems will remain unqualified. The registration process in its entirety represents a critical component of an interoperable application. It is as much a part of the system as any technical component and equally capable of introducing unwanted variations into real-time operations.

We have mentioned the need for commonality in interfaces and templates and highlighted the importance of the registration process. Yet there are more factors to consider if we wish to achieve true interoperability. One easily overlooked such factor is the consistency between biometric capture devices and their particular configuration. If there are significant variations in this respect, one device may verify an identity check, while a second device might refuse it, even though the same individual and same reference template are being employed. Clearly this would represent an undesirable state of affairs, especially as applications are scaled upwards in terms of numbers of users and transactions. We therefore need to specify not only the device itself but the limits of operational performance against a known benchmark. Each device must then be calibrated and tested accordingly and retested at defined intervals in order to maintain a minimum standard of operation. In certain situations, the physical environment may directly affect the operation of the biometric capture device, necessitating a degree of flexibility in order to be calibrated to the reference standard. In the context of a small closed-loop system, we may not be overly concerned with such issues, but within a wide-scale application, especially one deployed over multiple sites, this factor becomes very important indeed. Therefore, a methodology must be established and implemented in order to ensure the consistent operation of a number of devices over time. Some time ago, the author devised and created a system which enabled the automatic calibration of devices across boundaries of both time and geography via a centralised administration point, wherein a desired performance could be chosen and then every node on the system would automatically adjust its own parameters in order to maintain this performance criterion. This system, which was named APEX, was elegant and simple in concept and, with a little collaboration from device suppliers, easily deployed. However, even though this system was made freely available to government agencies, including operational software, it was, to the author's knowledge, never adopted. Consequently, the very problem that APEX found a workable solution remains to this day. This fact is recounted here in order to demonstrate that politics plays a large part in many large-scale systems, especially those within the public domain. This is precisely why so many of these systems have failed and why certain of them which are currently in operation continue to fail in their objectives, even though this reality is disguised as part of the propaganda surrounding the political motivation of their implementation. Consequently, those with an inclination to do so will readily find ways of defeating these systems (as has been periodically demonstrated by the author at various conferences). This is precisely why it is so important to understand the lower-level systems configuration and associated operational issues, in order to form a realistic appreciation of the overall situation.

Another situation that we must take into account is exception handling and fallback procedures for when exceptions occur or automated procedures fail. We may split this conveniently into two areas; firstly, exception handling processes for when a biometric identity check fails or a transaction fails to complete for some other reason connected with the user (e.g. mistakes in operation) and, secondly, fallback procedures for equipment or systems failure which renders the automated process, including the biometric identity check, inoperable. For any application we should of course consider such eventualities and create the necessary procedures accordingly. These should be built into training programmes and documented accordingly for ongoing support and maintenance purposes. The issue arises of course when we have parallel applications in different locations and being managed by different entities. In such a situation, in order to achieve true interoperability, we must be confident that there is parity of operation at either end with regard to exception handling and fallback procedures. This is analogous with the need to also have complementary registration procedures. For true interoperability, we must be able to consider the application conceptually as a whole, even if it is dispersed across several locations and operated by several different entities.

We may appreciate from the above that true interoperability requires more than the use of comparable devices at different operational nodes. We have to strive to provide a common operational performance, including supporting processes, at any point within the broader application. This is of particular importance when considering large-scale applications in the public domain, such as might be the case in the provision of government services to citizens. In this context, the reader is referred to the Biometrics Constitution and Biometrics Charter documents which, together, provide a framework of understanding within which a system may be conceived, designed and implemented in a repeatable and sustainable manner. Furthermore, if these guidelines are followed, interaction with users will become considerably enhanced.

2.5 Understanding Infrastructural Issues

Operational infrastructures will be particular to the application in question. In most cases there will exist a well-defined architecture of network components and protocols, application servers, databases, operating systems, front-end clients and everything necessary to support the operation of the application. In tandem with this technical infrastructure, there will be an infrastructure of processes, the two together supporting the required functionality of the application. We may surmise that, especially in the case of an existing application, adding the functionality of a biometric identity check will not prove too burdensome to the existing infrastructure. However, this may or may not be the case, depending upon the precise design and functionality of the application at hand.

There are some fundamental factors to establish in this respect, the most obvious perhaps being the location of the reference biometric template. The primary choices here are storing the template once on a portable token such as a chip card, storing the template in a central database, storing the template within a distributed database (possibly held within a network of devices) or a combination of these approaches. One can immediately appreciate that, in the case of a multi-node or multisite application, there will be a network overhead if we store reference templates within a central database. In such a model, there is also the security and integrity of the template to consider as it is passed between systems and network components. If we are anticipating large databases, as might be the case for applications in the public domain, then we shall also have to consider the secure replication of such a database from both an operational and disaster recovery perspective. We shall also need to carefully consider the administration of such a database from both a sustainability and data integrity perspective. This will require the establishment of, and adherence to, a strong set of rules and procedures which are themselves derived from an overarching policy. In addition to the management of biometric data within a networked model, we must also consider where the matching of the live and reference data will take place. This may occur within the biometric capture device itself or remotely via a software 'engine' running the appropriate algorithm. It may even be undertaken on a portable device which is in wireless communication with the host application. The application developer has potentially many ways of arranging this according to the devices and software modules being employed. In the interests of simplicity and efficiency, many will prefer to keep the reference template on a portable token, read this token at the capture device node and undertake the match between the reference and live sample within the biometric device/terminal itself, simply transmitting a 'match' or 'non-match' result to the host system. Indeed, it is now possible with some techniques to undertake the match on the chip card itself, thus never transferring a copy of the template into another subsystem. There are obvious security-related benefits of such an approach.

A variation upon this theme would be to store the reference template on the token as before and read this template via a token reader but then undertake the matching process within the host application, away from the device. Some favour such an approach, believing that it offers a degree of protection against either tampering with the biometric device or otherwise injecting a 'passed' result into the host application. The downside of course is that we are now transferring both the reference template and the live biometric data across the network to wherever the host application and matching engine sit. Furthermore, if we allow the user more than one attempt to provide good-quality live biometric data, then several instances of transferring such data across the network for each transaction may ensue. This may not be perceived as a problem within a small-scale closed-loop application but may quickly become an issue within a very large-scale application, for which there will be network capacity and performance issues to understand. The choice between these two approaches may be further suggested by the availability of suitably proven hardware and software. Several biometric device manufacturers chose to undertake the matching process within the host software rather than within the device. This of course makes it easier to implement software revisions such as improvements in the matching algorithm itself.

Some application designers will prefer a client-server database model where either the live biometric data is transported to a central position and matched there or the reference template is transported to the remote node for matching against the live sample. If we are anticipating a one-to-one match, then it may make sense to keep this activity at the remote node. If we are anticipating a one-to-many match, then this of course has to happen at a database position, either centrally located or distributed. It should be acknowledged that different biometric techniques display varying abilities to match on a one-to-many basis, returning differing levels of performance accordingly. Not all are particularly well suited to this mode of operation. At the present time, iris recognition has potential advantages in this respect as, with appropriate iris codes, certain implementations can match a live sample against a large number of reference templates in an efficient manner and in close to real time. In small- and medium-scale applications, this has certainly proved to be the case and there are now a number of large-scale applications employing this technique. On the other side of the coin, facial recognition is not so suited to such an approach at the current time (when matching against a live sample) as it is likely to generate a high number of false matches if the matching threshold is set to offer reasonable protection against false non-matches. At this juncture we should acknowledge the distinction between real-time biometric operation against a live sample and pattern matching one stored facial image against another offline as is being increasingly undertaken for a variety of purposes. In the latter instance one might be prepared to accept a high percentage of false matches, depending upon the precise nature of the application and the processes in place to manage such a situation.

Another option might be where a token is employed, but the token does not contain the reference biometric template. Instead it is used to retrieve a specific template from a central database by the use of a unique identifier which is linked to the data record for the individual to whom the token was issued. Thus, when presenting the token the individual is effectively claiming an identity and providing his or her live biometric data to be verified against the centrally held reference template. In such a model we have the same issue of transferring biometric data across a network, either with the template travelling from the host application to the operational node, or vice versa, depending upon precisely where the match is to be undertaken. If the token should fall into the wrong hands, or copies are made for illegal purposes, then the likelihood of an impostor being able to falsely claim the identity and associated benefit will depend upon the performance of the biometric matching process. If the technique employed has a relatively poor false acceptance rate, then this may encourage such impostor attempts. The reader will now be considering the likelihood of being able to copy the legitimate user's biometric trait, perhaps by manufacturing a false finger or hand or replicating the appearance of the face. Such practices have of course been tried by the biometric fraternity in order to understand the risk of this happening. When using mathematically derived templates in association with liveness testing at the device position, the risk is generally accepted to be quite low. The impostor in question would have to be quite determined to go to so much trouble in order to pretend to be someone else, not to say that this will not occasionally occur. The careful application designer will incorporate additional checks in order to guard against this, especially in a high-security situation. An alternative approach is considered whereupon the token is used to retrieve a specific template from the database and matching is undertaken within the host application. In this instance, the reference templates may be securely managed, but we are of course transmitting the live biometric data across the network, possibly more than once for each transaction. We shall need to ensure that this data is protected accordingly.

We have so far explored various ways of using a token in association with a biometric identity check. This is absolutely valid as, in many cases, this will be the preferred mode of operation, especially as the token may hold other demographic information pertinent to the core application and perhaps other applications besides. For example, a national identity card may incorporate a biometric or be otherwise used in an application requiring biometric identity checks, but it may also be used for other purposes and perhaps within other applications. We can therefore expect to see many such models. However, with certain biometric techniques, we may decide not to use a token at all and rely upon the system operating in identification mode, i.e. matching a live biometric against a database of reference templates without the user claiming a specific identity.

Such an approach may seem attractive from many perspectives, depending on the nature and functionality of the application. As previously mentioned though, the ability to operate in this mode, particularly with large databases, will depend very much upon the biometric technique employed. With such a model, we shall also have to carefully consider the overall systems architecture and how to ensure reliable and consistent operation from perhaps multiple operational points generating potentially large numbers of transactions. We may choose to replicate such a database for reasons of both efficiency and security, in which case a robust process for achieving this must be established, including the necessary synchronisation between the replicated copies. In this respect, a closer integration with existing server and client operating systems and database technologies may be appropriate.

We might usefully acknowledge that infrastructural issues are not necessarily restricted to purely technical matters. The registration process once again becomes pertinent as we consider our infrastructural design. If we intend to create the reference template directly upon the portable token and nowhere else, then we can establish appropriate procedures via stand-alone nodes for this purpose. If, on the other hand, we are storing the templates within a central database (which we shall in any case wish to do for backup purposes), then we shall have to consider the real-time database administration implications, including the communications link and administrator access rights. In this respect, we would be foolish to overlook the scalability issue. Interfacing with a remote database from a handful of nodes and in the context of a few dozen transactions may seem quite straightforward. Extend this to many hundreds of nodes and hundreds of thousands of transactions and the situation becomes a little more complex. Add to this real-time parallel operation and we can appreciate that there will be some infrastructural design challenges to meet for this type of application.

While we are on the subject of operational infrastructures, we must consider the possibility of using digital certificates within a public key infrastructure (PKI) in order to confirm the biometric template as authentic and restrict access to it to authorised systems and processes. There are many champions of such an approach and, it seems, equally many who are passionately against this methodology. Those in favour proclaim the virtues of using certificates and keys for additional security in authenticating the biometric template and securing its passage from point to point. Those against bemoan the additional complexity of such an approach and doubt that it would be manageable in relation to very large and complex applications. We should also acknowledge the commercial reality, in that many of the proponents have aspirations to set themselves up as a third-party trusted certificate authority. Those against will be ready to point to the failure of this model for even smaller-scale applications and the potential muddle that can result. It is indeed a contentious situation. If we adopt a pragmatic approach, we may conclude that there are theoretical advantages to the use of certificates and keys with biometric templates but that these may be offset against the inherent complexity and sustainability in the case of large-scale distributed applications. We might also reason that a properly designed application with equally robust operational processes can work perfectly well outside of a PKI. It is certainly an area that needs to be evaluated with great care. Part of this evaluation should address both initial and ongoing costs and part of it should address practical interoperability issues, especially if an application is to be shared between administrations. In any event, the PKI approach has been followed with respect to chip passports and associated readers, ensuring that sensitive information on the chip may only be read by authorised processes, and this is being managed perfectly well. Whether such an approach is suitable for other applications may be a matter of evaluating risks and benefits, as with any proposed initiative.

Perhaps a good approach to the whole infrastructure question would be to start with the most simplistic model (probably the biometric template being stored on a portable token and matched within the biometric device, without the help of digital certificates and keys) and then ask why this wouldn't work for your particular application. If there is a valid reason, then by all means, we may gradually add layers of sophistication until a workable and satisfactory solution has been arrived at. This would seem a more realistic approach than starting with a highly complex model on the basis of theoretically improved security and then finding it unmanageable in the real world. For each application there will be an optimum infrastructural model which can be realistically deployed and maintained. Identifying this model is part of good application design but will require a broad understanding of the functional requirements of the application in question, together with the technical and architectural realities of deployment and ongoing maintenance and support. A good approach would be to identify and document all of the associated data flows within the broader system, aligning them with potential security risks and associated probabilities of failure. One may then ensure that the underlying infrastructure is designed in such a manner as to be secure, robust and reliable. Operational performance will also be important and one must allow for scalability beyond the immediate requirement, especially when designing the network and associated components. In addition, depending upon the application software design, one must be cognisant of version dependencies and interactions between components and services. This situation should be fully documented for ongoing support and maintenance purposes. Unfortunately, within our modern IT-centric world and its fast pace of change, this factor is becoming increasingly pertinent.

Human Factors

3

We have discussed at some length the relevant technical factors associated with the deployment of applications which incorporate an automated biometric identity check, but there are other factors to take into account in this context. Primary among these are perhaps human factors. You may consider that human factors are mostly associated with system usability or individual capability and certainly these are important points to consider, but there is more to it than that. Human factors can have a direct and significant impact upon operational systems performance. They should also figure prominently when designing attendant processes for exception handling, registration and, indeed, the functionality and operation of the whole application. We are, after all, considering applications in which humans play a very significant part; otherwise, why would we be considering automated biometric identity checks? If the identity of the individual is critical to our application, then so is the manner in which the individual interfaces with the application. This is not just a matter of systems usability, although this is a factor which will be discussed later. It is an altogether more complex area, but one which is important to understand if we are to implement successful applications of this kind. We shall therefore in this chapter consider the human factor element with special regard to the use of biometrics. For purposes of clarity, we have subdivided this area into distinct sections. User psychology looks at the importance of individual characteristics, scalability and usability with regard to human factors. It is recognised that the human element is as much a part of systems design as is the technical architecture of a given application. Furthermore, human factors play a direct and significant role in realised systems performance, a reality which remains poorly understood in some circles.

© Springer-Verlag London 2015
J. Ashbourn, *Practical Biometrics*, DOI 10.1007/978-1-4471-6717-4_3

3.1   User Psychology

The concept of user psychology in relation to biometrics was first introduced by the author in the mid-1990s, initially in the form of a tabular scoring method with which to modify the published performance figures of a given device or system in order to more reasonably reflect real operational situations. It was devised partly in response to the continually observed disparity between theoretical and realised performance and partly to encourage a better understanding of how user psychology factors can have a direct impact upon operational performance. This mechanism was later transformed into a simple software utility and further refined into the User Psychology wizard which is freely available online from the Biometrics Research website (details of how to use this software are covered elsewhere in this book).

When we speak of user psychology, we are referring to a fairly broad area of possible conditions and variations which affect the way in which human beings behave in a particular situation, just as in the even broader area of general psychology. Similarly, as with commonly understood human psychology, variations in individual mood, attitude or state of health may result in direct physiological change, thus depending upon the biometric technique used, compounding an already complex situation when seeking to match a live sample with a previously captured reference. Furthermore, user psychology factors are relevant not just in everyday operation but throughout the whole project, including the initial communication to prospective users and their subsequent registration into the system. Let's explore this more fully.

We can start by recognising that users may or may not have preconceived ideas about the use of biometrics for automated identity checks. They may have serious doubts about both the technology and the real intentions behind its use, especially if it is a government-controlled public system. They may also have legitimate concerns over how their personal biometric data is stored and used. If they are starting off from this perspective, they are unlikely to be enthusiastic users of the system, even if its use is compulsory. Consequently, they will make little effort to use the system properly and will probably be happy enough should the system fail. In such a situation, we have a significant communications task before us, in order to properly answer such concerns and explain clearly the use of the system and its perceived benefits. This is the first step in managing user psychology. Note that mistakes made at this point will certainly have repercussions further along the line. If there are genuine concerns from the proposed user base, we must strive to fully investigate these concerns and establish operational architectures and processes which properly address them. This must then be clearly communicated in sufficient detail for users to understand the infrastructural operation, including how their biometric data is used, by whom and for what purpose. In certain situations, there will be data protection legislation to consider and to ensure compliance with. Having got this far, we should give the proposed user base an opportunity to comment and ask any other questions they may have in relation to the project. Indeed, we may have to do this more than once depending upon the nature and scale of the project. If all of this is managed properly and sincerely, we should now have a user base who properly understands the proposed application, why it is being established, how it will work and how it affects them as individuals. There may still be some who remain fundamentally opposed to such a development but, hopefully, these will now represent a small minority. To aid this all-important stage at the formation of an initiative, the Biometrics Constitution and Biometrics Charter Document will prove invaluable to both systems designers and operating agencies. The former will provide guidance on many aspects which are not typically covered by systems designers and consultants, while the latter provides for an unambiguous communication vehicle with which to involve prospective users. The two documents are freely available from the Biometrics Research website and should play a key role in every application development which involves biometric identity verification. Their active usage is thus highly recommended.

However, the requirement for good and honest communication doesn't stop there. We must carry this over to the registration process itself and ensure that every user understands exactly what is happening, why the process works as it does and what they should do in order to register in a satisfactory manner. Note that this is not just a question of the biometric enrolment, but the whole process including prior identity authentication by whatever means has been decided upon. By now the user should have a good understanding of why the application is being introduced, how it works and what they need to do personally to enrol. They will therefore mostly be in a positive state of mind and probably quite intrigued about the technology itself, especially if they have never used biometrics before. This provides a customer service-related opportunity to build upon this factor and take special care to explain the enrolment process and help them through it in order to create a high-quality biometric template for each individual. It also provides an opportunity to dispel myths and answer questions about the biometric technology being used. From a subsequent operational perspective, high-quality templates are obviously highly desirable if reliable operation is to be expected. Imagine now a different scenario, where users have not been given adequate information about why the application is being introduced and how it works. Furthermore, they have been given no opportunity to air their views, ask questions or have any involvement in the situation prior to arriving for registration. What frame of mind will they be in? As individuals, they will probably represent quite a mixed bunch. Some of them are enthusiastic and eager to take part, some of them are suspicious and not particularly interested, and some of them are openly hostile and determined not to be cooperative, even if use of the system is mandatory. How variable will the quality of templates be under such a scenario? Probably substantially so, with the attendant effect upon subsequent operational performance. We could establish a quality threshold, below which the individual would have to re-enrol. In the above scenario, if we need to re-enrol (sometimes several times) a percentage of unenthusiastic individuals, this could have a significant impact upon costs and operational time scales. You may now reasonably ask the question about remote enrolment, perhaps over the Internet or via kiosks at designated locations. Certainly this may be feasible for some users, providing proper communication has taken place and the on-screen user feedback and operational process are of the highest standard. However, if there is no human being in attendance, then an opportunity is missed to positively manage user psychology.

Furthermore, the variance in quality of enrolled reference templates will likely be significant. In general, one would not recommend remote enrolment or self-enrolment as, in addition to technical considerations, there is the problem of verifying the identity of the user prior to registration. This is a task best undertaken by an experienced and qualified human being. With respect to large-scale public projects, the possibility of outsourcing the registration process will probably occur to many. This would also not be recommended as experience shows us that the probability of realising a high-quality service via committed and skilled operational staff is extremely low under such a model. Furthermore the opportunities for registering false identities, intentionally or otherwise, would be enhanced and very real. Such a model could also have the effect of making users feel somewhat remote from the core application and therefore somewhat less than enthusiastic about its operation. The implementing agency, whether in the private or public sectors, should take full responsibility for the design, implementation and ongoing operation of the end-to-end application, including user registration. They should similarly be responsible for systems security and data management, ensuring compliance with all in-place privacy and data protection legislation.

Having focused on the situation prior to actual operation and seen that user psychology might be usefully understood and managed, let us now turn our attention to the variables of real-time operation. Even given perfect environmental and operational conditions (which, of course, never actually exist), there are various factors which might affect the way in which the user interfaces with the system and the resulting performance of the transaction, for example, the degree of confidence that the user has as to their own ability to use the system properly. It may be that this is their first real transaction under live operational conditions. Or it may be that they are an infrequent user and are worried that they will not remember the correct operational process. If, in addition, there is a queue of other users behind them, they may feel additional pressure, especially if they are of a naturally shy disposition. Compare this scenario with an individual who is a frequent user of the system and very confident of both the operational process and their own ability to undertaken a successful transaction. These two users will certainly act differently and will provide a more or less consistent sample of their live biometrics for comparison against the reference template. The time window necessary to complete the entire transaction will be quite different for these two users. Consider another scenario whereby the user is late for an appointment, had trouble finding the operational point of presence and then found a sizeable queue. Consider further that this particular user was not enthusiastic about the application in the first place and that when he uses the system, an error occurs and he is denied access. He tries again with the same result and, meanwhile, a queue is forming behind him. He criticises the application loudly and is becoming angry. He tries a third time, very clumsily giving his biometrics, and is rejected once more. The likelihood of this particular individual undertaking a successful transaction is becoming increasingly weak, as he becomes more and more agitated and less and less likely to provide his biometrics in the precise manner necessary for a good match. He may also have undergone some slight physiological change. His hands may be sweating. His pupils may have dilated. His facial expression will have changed. Depending upon the biometric technique employed and the precise calibration of the biometric capture device, this may also have an impact upon systems performance. Multiply these effects by thousands of users across tens or hundreds of transaction points and you can start to appreciate what this may mean for your overall transactional error rates and, consequently, the perceived operational success of the application. In reaction to such a situation, an implementing agency will be tempted to simply lower the matching threshold of the system, allowing users to be accepted even when providing little consistency in their usage pattern. This, in turn, will raise the probability of false acceptance quite considerably, thus negating the objectives of the application. This is exactly what has happened in some quite high-profile situations. It is also a scenario which illustrates the weakness of a fixed matching threshold for all users. This point will be discussed elsewhere in the book.

We have described one way in which user psychology may be affected by operational scenarios and may, in turn, affect the correct operation of the system and thus overall system performance. There are other factors to consider, one of which is the operational environment itself. Variables such as ambient temperature, quality of lighting, occupational density and even the attractiveness of the immediate surroundings and décor can all affect the way an individual feels and therefore approaches the system. Environmental factors can also directly affect the operation of the biometric capture devices. Variables such as temperature, humidity and lighting can all have an effect. Add the equipment variances to the human variances and you have an interesting potential for errors. If an individual frequently experiences errors, they will start to lose confidence in the system and will be almost expecting it not to work. In such a frame of mind, the likelihood of an error will be increased in proportion to the users' ability to consistently provide a good-quality biometric sample. The more errors they experience, the less likely they are to be consistent in the way they provide their biometric and the less they will heed the advice originally given to them about usage. Eventually, they may need to re-enrol and/or be retrained in the correct use of the system. This may not be a problem in relation to a small self-contained application but may represent a significant problem for a large multisite application, possibly administered by multiple agencies. Of course, there will always be transactional exceptions and one must establish a suitable process for handling them. If these exceptions represent a very low percentage of overall transactions, they may be comfortably managed. If this percentage starts to creep up, the situation will naturally become more difficult to manage. If users experience increasing usage errors and notice that these exceptions are not being managed well, their perception of the application will suffer which, in turn, has an impact upon user psychology. Such a situation has the makings of a vicious circle which may be difficult or costly to control, especially if we are dealing with large-scale public applications. We can appreciate therefore that managing user psychology with respect to applications which feature automated biometric identity checks, is an important factor with respect to successful operation. In order to manage this factor, we must first understand it and the ways in which it might impact overall systems performance. Each application will of course be slightly different and we cannot prescribe cause and effect to a high degree of accuracy within a generic context. The program manager for the application in question must understand the user base, the operational environment and all the factors which can influence the manner in which users may interact with the application. The User Psychology wizard provides a useful first step in establishing such an understanding and is consequently recommended.

3.2   Individual Characteristics

This is a subject likely to excite debate as we touch upon areas such as ethnicity, ageing, relative health and gender. The question remains as to how much these factors might affect the operation of different biometric techniques. There are several views on the subject, some more aligned with practical experience than others, but relatively little in the way of qualified research. However, it has become clear from experience that individual characteristics can, under some circumstances, make a difference to the biometric verification process. At the most basic level, physical size can have an effect. For example, smaller or larger than average hands and fingertips may be difficult to align with hand readers and fingerprint readers. An individual shorter or taller in stature than average may find it difficult to align with a camera used for facial recognition or iris scanning if its positioning has not been properly considered. It follows also that individuals with physical disability may find it hard to use certain biometric devices. Note that such a physical disability need not be extreme. For example, an individual with arthritis may find it quite difficult to use devices based upon the hand or fingers. Many individuals suffer with back and neck problems which reduce movement and may cause similar difficulties in aligning with biometric transducers. In certain cases, individuals with physiological inconsistencies will not even be able to enrol their biometric trait. Within a well-conceived application, we naturally need to make allowances for these exceptions and ensure that affected individuals are not inadvertently discriminated against as a result of an inadequately designed system or related process.

Notwithstanding the obvious physical conditions referred to above, let us consider some of the other individual factors, however awkward this may be. First of all is gender. Is there any evidence to suggest that males and females have subtly different biometric traits or have different probabilities of being able to use certain biometric techniques? There are views both for and against this contention. On the one hand, it is clear that females tend to have smaller hands and fingertips (and, in many cultures, tend to maintain longer fingernails) which may or may not affect the practical use of finger- or hand-based devices. But what about irises and retinas? Some maintain that there is a difference although, to date, there seems to have been little qualified medical or biological research on this point. There are of course subtle differences in the voice production mechanisms of males and females which, while perhaps typically producing a different waveform profile for a given phrase, do not seem to affect the operation of voice verification systems. When it comes to facial recognition, it may be that females are more likely to superficially alter their appearance with cosmetics and different hairstyles from time to time, and this may well affect the performance of some facial recognition systems, but this does not in itself suggest any greater or lesser probability of likeness between samples. In fact, when dealing with gender, we might usefully distinguish between obvious differences in size and appearance and physiological or psychological differences which may have an impact upon biometric verification performance. For example, while females may typically have smaller or more slender fingertips than males, is there a difference in the predominance of fingerprint types, which may affect biometric operation? Do female eyes have different characteristics or fall into different groupings compared with male eyes? Is the bone structure of female skulls different enough to make a difference for our purposes? It's a difficult subject for, on the one hand, we clearly need more qualified research in order to answer some of these questions while, on the other hand, there does seem to be a small body of opinion to suggest that gender may be of some significance. The problem is this opinion is rarely supported by undisputed statistical evidence. On balance, there clearly are physiological differences between males and females. To what degree this might affect the operation of biometric identity verification remains to be ascertained. This factor may assume greater importance with scale and the wise program manager for a large-scale application will certainly address this question.

Age is another factor for which there are divided opinions in this context. There are perhaps two broad areas within which to collate our thinking. Firstly, there is the rate of physiological change associated with the ageing process. Secondly, there is the affect of ageing upon the biometric traits commonly used for biometric identity verification. With respect to the former, there would seem to be a consensus that rate of change is more pronounced at either end of the age scale with a period of greater stability in the middle range. Thus, adolescents clearly undergo fairly rapid change in their teenage years, and at the other end of the scale, there typically comes a time when change starts to accelerate, often from the early or middle 60s onwards. The latter parameter is more difficult to pin down as there seems to be a wider difference among individuals at this end of the spectrum. Of course, the primary effect that these changes have upon the operation of biometric verification systems is one of poor template matching, as the live biometric may vary increasingly from the reference sample (there may also be user psychology differentials to add to the equation). This may necessitate re-enrolment, perhaps a number of times over a given period, or with increased frequency for individuals at either end of the age spectrum. It is a factor to take into consideration when planning the logistics of a large-scale application and it can, of course, be managed by constantly revising the reference template with each successful live comparison. However, this approach introduces other issues. The other question is precisely how the ageing process might affect the biometric trait. It is held in some circles for example that fingerprints become less distinct as the skin becomes more brittle. Furthermore, minor damage to the fingertips may take a little longer to heal. Irises are thought not to change significantly with age, although interfacing with the iris recognition camera device may become more difficult for some individuals at the extremes of the age scale. Facial appearance clearly does alter with age, more so in some individuals than others, and this may necessitate re-enrolment into such a system. Hand geometry may also change slightly, although the primary hand geometry technology has the capability to be constantly revising the reference template with each transaction, providing an automatic tracking of slowly changing individual characteristics. There is little doubt that individual ageing will eventually have an effect upon the reliable operation of biometric identity verification transactions. This may easily be managed by incorporating suitable processes to ensure that individuals have the opportunity to refresh their reference biometric templates at suitable intervals. For many, this may not be necessary for some considerable time. However, in certain applications, a proportion of the user base is likely to be approaching a time in their lives when physiological changes due the ageing process start to accelerate. We must acknowledge this reality and design our applications accordingly. We might also usefully acknowledge that, with respect to a diverse user base containing all age ranges, a single matching threshold is unlikely to work well across such a range of transactions.

Ethnicity is an area likely to be controversial, at least in some respects. Clearly, ethnicity often manifests itself in physical appearance, but does this also have an effect upon the popular biometric traits and the resulting operational performance? This is another area where some interesting and sometimes opposing views exist and where we could use a little more qualified research and statistical evidence. If we start with the face, as humans, we can clearly and quickly classify individual ethnicity, at least as far as the major groupings are concerned. But does this make it any easier or harder to distinguish individuals from within the same ethnic group? From our own recognition perspective, much depends upon familiarity with the group in question. If we rarely find ourselves in the company of individuals from a specific ethnic group for example, we may find it harder to distinguish between individuals of similar appearance from within that particular group. However, if we spend 6 months working with such a group, our abilities in this direction will no doubt quickly increase. Familiarity obviously has a part to play here. Facial recognition technology however does not work in quite the same way as the human brain. There are variations in approach, but mostly the technology is interested in the pattern it sees before it and how similar this pattern is to the pattern of the reference template or image. Factors such as the eye centres, relative position of the mouth and nose or boundary of the image according to a pixel-based evaluation will be important. Given that variations of skin colour against a known background and under controlled lighting conditions should be largely understood, the question becomes one of individual genetic similarity within a given group. Experience with very large and ethnically mixed user bases may provide us with some answers as we move ahead, but we should be wary of making assumptions. Irises among different ethnic groups look quite different to us, but iris recognition technology usually finds sufficient detail to create a usable reference template. There are very occasional exceptions whereby an individual is unable to enrol to an acceptable standard (failure to enrol) although this has not been conclusively linked to ethnicity. Occlusion of the iris can sometimes be an issue, and this tends to vary among ethnic groups, but is by no means exclusive in this respect. Once again we need the benefit of experience and qualified research in order to be able to form proper conclusions. With regard to fingerprints, it is understood that the propensity of different fingerprint patterns varies among the primary ethnic groups, although how this translates to operational performance is not quite so clear. Much may depend upon the biometric fingerprint technique employed, for example, whether it is minutiae- or pattern-based and how the matching threshold has been configured. Skin texture and the relative definition of fingerprints may vary slightly, but occupational activities are likely to play a larger part in altering the visible fingerprint in this respect, for example, those employed in activities where abrasive contact is unavoidable or perhaps where contact with certain chemical compounds has an effect. Certain implementations of biometric fingerprint reading technology claim to read slightly beneath the visible surface and are therefore less affected by such variables. It is likely that there will be a small number of failure to enrol instances with fingerprint technology as with other biometric techniques, although, with potentially ten fingers to choose from, the individual user may have a relatively high probability of finding at least one usable digit. Voice verification represents an interesting area here, not so much because of known physiological differences among ethnic groups but because of the language spoken by the individual and the resulting different emphasis on certain sounds. A phrase of the same meaning spoken in different languages can produce a very different sound, both audibly and when captured and viewed as a waveform. The relative dynamics of the spoken phrase may differ considerably, perhaps providing more or less granularity for the biometric algorithm to work with. This does not seem to present too many problems in practice, although a very large user population of mixed ethnicity and spoken language may present some interesting challenges to the configuration of a typical voice verification application, including bandwidth and sensitivity settings.

We have briefly mentioned disabilities in the context of physical disabilities which may themselves be of a temporary, permanent or progressive nature. However, not all disabilities are immediately visible or indeed physical. Many individuals have nonphysical disabilities such as learning difficulty, varying degrees of autism and other conditions which may render a consistent interaction with biometric devices more difficult for them than for others. Within fully automated systems, it is impossible to distinguish whether such conditions are the cause of operational errors. We shall simply be generating transactional errors without understanding the root cause. This is precisely why, even in respect of automated systems, human attendance should always be included within the overall design. In the case of non-obvious disabilities, it provides the opportunity for individuals to be assisted where required and in a sympathetic manner. It also allows for an understanding of the effects of user psychology upon realised performance to be studied and understood. In addition, in times of system malfunction or other extraordinary condition, a human administrator may quickly take control and may make operational decisions accordingly.

In summary, individual characteristics as discussed above are bound to have some effect upon the efficacy of automated biometric identity verification. The question is the degree of this effect and whether it is sufficient to cause significant operational variations. In a relatively small closed-loop application with a known user base of perhaps largely similar individual types, this is unlikely to be a significant issue. However, when we move into the territory of large user bases featuring considerable diversity of age, gender, ethnicity, physical robustness and other variables, then the issues may become more pronounced and start to affect operational reliability. We must therefore take such factors into consideration, striving to fully understand our users and the effects of variations of user psychology upon the practical operation and realised performance of our overall application. Herein lies the distinction between systems which incorporate biometric identity verification and those which do not. With the former, the user effectively becomes a systems component, interacting with other systems components within the broader data flow. Consequently, a degree of unpredictability is introduced, as a consequence of the human condition. The concept of User Psychology, as developed and refined by the author over many years, provides a measure as to the expected variance of realised performance aligned with certain combinations of situation and user type. An awareness of User Psychology and its effects will greatly aid the intelligent design of applications, including the underlying technical infrastructure and the attendant operational processes.

3.3   Scalability

Scalability is often considered from the technical infrastructure perspective where, indeed, it is an important factor to understand. It also has a relevance from the human factor point of view where the importance of understanding the effects of scale should not be underestimated. We can see this right at the beginning in how you reach and communicate with prospective users. In a closed-loop environment such as a small- or medium-sized organisation, it is relatively easy to communicate a new idea or mode of operation to all those involved. However, extrapolate this to large numbers across multiple sites and the task becomes a little more complex. Extrapolate again to a prospective user base the size of a national population and you have a major operation on your hands which will require a great deal of planning and coordination. One may readily appreciate how scalability becomes important. If we now take this national population-sized user base and consider how we are going to liaise with them personally in order to gather and process whatever information is required, we have a more complex logistical problem to consider. Administration itself becomes a major issue in communicating with a user base of this size. If we are considering the implementation of a biometric identity check in various public applications which involve the majority of the population, then we have to consider the registration process very carefully. Again, there is a huge distinction between registering a biometric for a few hundred people in a commercial organisation and registering perhaps tens of millions of people in a public application. There will be a balance to consider between the number of registration points of presence and the time required to register tens of millions of individuals. Of course, before you can enrol anyone into your application, you will need a sufficient number of fully trained personnel who understand the biometric enrolment process in depth and can facilitate at purpose-designed registration centres. It will take time to train these operators to the required standard and this commitment will be directly proportional to the number of users anticipated for your application. You may consider phasing such an operation over an extended period of time, but this approach has additional implications in running parallel operations and processes for longer than may be necessary, at least in relation to the initial phase of a given operation.

Scalability as applied to human factors is also very relevant from a real-time operational perspective. Assume that we now have everyone registered and biometrically enrolled for our large-scale application. We shall have to now provide exception handling processes on an equivalent scale. Consider the differences once again between an application with 1 or 200 users and an application with perhaps 70 million users. Depending upon the number of transactions across a defined number of points of presence, the instances of operational errors in relation to the automated biometric identity check are going to be proportionally increased. Whatever our exception handling processes are, we are going to have to provide for them on a large scale. This in turn requires a greater number of trained operators. It may well be that existing personnel can be retrained to undertake such a process, but we have to allow for this in our planning and understand the potential impact of such a course of action on day-to-day operations. Indeed, the entire administration around such a large-scale application will need to be of a sufficient scale to guarantee reliable operation and the efficient processing of exceptions and, where appropriate, issues raised by users. There will be operational complexities relating to the biometric verification process that existing personnel will simply not understand and for which they will require training. It may be useful to take a close look at some of the pilot systems and trials that have been undertaken, where automated biometric identity checks have featured as part of the operation. If we consider what it took, just from the human factor perspective, to get everything running smoothly with a user base of a given size and then extrapolate this effort to a considerably larger user base, we shall start to understand scalability in this light. However, even this approach is likely to underestimate the real human factor requirements when dealing with applications for use by national populations. There are logistical and managerial issues for very large-scale applications which simply do not exist in smaller operations. This factor of scalability is one which we must consider very seriously indeed. From a technical perspective, we must also consider how matching algorithms apply to a large, potentially mixed, user base. The one-size-fits-all approach employed in the majority of systems inevitably means that, in real terms, the system will be configured for the lowest common denominator and may, in reality, not be delivering anything like the performance claimed for it. Bearing in mind also that, in the case of false positives, we shall not even know about the vast majority of such errors or whether certain individuals are repeatedly defeating the system. As operations scale upwards, this becomes more of an issue. In the case of a truly large-scale application, such concerns must also be aligned with the objectives of the operation, including the perceived risks involved. In some instances, it may be considered that matching accuracy is not actually that important and that the psychological effect of the presence of such systems is enough. In instances where matching accuracy is considered important, then there are many factors to take into consideration and much to understand about what a biometric match or non-match is really telling us. Many implementing agencies have yet to develop a robust understanding in this context.

3.4   Usability

In any activity and in any walk of life, the way in which we interface as individuals with machinery and technology is very important. A housewife using a kitchen blender may enjoy using it, or positively hate using it, depending upon its ergonomic and practical design. A truck driver may distinctly prefer a certain make of truck because of its ergonomics and the resulting ease with which it may be driven over long distances. A musician will be attracted to a particular instrument which suits their particular style of playing and with which they feel comfortable. An office administrator will either love or hate a particular software program according to its look and feel and how logical its operation is perceived to be. It is quite natural for human beings to consider any physical entity with which they are required to interface in terms of its usability. Furthermore, research has shown us that their own performance when using the physical entity can be affected in direct proportion to their perception of how usable this entity is. If the interface is difficult for them as an individual, they will consider the entity a poor one and will come to expect poor performance when using it. If the interface works well for them personally, they will consider the entity a good one and will enjoy using it. This in turn will boost their own confidence and almost certainly result in a better achieved performance overall. There is of course a strong element of user psychology at play here as individuals form opinions about the devices with which they need to interface as part of their everyday lives and why they need to do so.

Within the context of our large-scale application, usability is important in several key areas. First of all, from the users' perspective, if the user is required to interface with the system in order to provide a live biometric sample, then this process needs to be highly intuitive. The user must be absolutely clear as to what they are supposed to do and should receive logical feedback and, where appropriate, instruction at every point along the way. In addition, the interface from their perspective should be attractive and inviting. Indeed, it should be such that they positively want to use it and enjoy undertaking each transaction accordingly. Sadly, this has not been the case with many of the biometric schemes implemented to date. Perhaps this hasn't been considered as such an important factor but, in fact, it is a very important factor to consider if we seek smoothly operating applications with user bases of significant proportions. The issue manifests itself at several levels. Firstly, there is the biometric capture device itself. Device manufacturers have probably been too concerned with the technical performance of their product to worry too much about ergonomics and usability. One only has to look at some of the fingerprint readers currently on the market to see the truth of this. It is a great shame, as a little creative thought could achieve much in this respect and would help towards a better realised transactional performance. Even noncontact techniques, such as iris and facial recognition, require a clearly defined user interface. In all cases, we must consider how feedback is provided to the user, which may be partly a function of the capture device itself and partly a function of the associated software and operational environment. The interface needs to be inviting and crystal clear in terms of guiding the user through the operational process. There must be no ambiguity or confusion. Exception handling must be particularly well considered and must leave the user feeling comfortable at all times, even in the case of rejection. The physical manifestation of the overall interface, whether it be via a kiosk or some other physical arrangement, is also very important if the user is to be made comfortable with the overall operational process, as is the immediate physical environment. This state of affairs is not difficult to achieve and yet we so rarely see really good examples of usability in relation to operational systems or even singular software packages. The Internet provides us with some interesting examples. The variability of websites with respect to their user interface and consequent usability is huge. Some sites, even from otherwise well-respected organisations, are simply dreadful in terms of their operational logic and lack of intuitive design. It is as if everything has been designed around the wishes of the supplier and not the consumer, a modern trend which leads to a good deal of dissatisfaction. This applies similarly with mainstream software packages. I am writing this book on a computer which has perhaps the three most popular word processors available on it. They are all flawed in one way or another, even after many years of supposedly constant development. They are not short of features, many of which I shall never use, but I yearn for a more logical and usable interface and the ability to easily undertake the primary tasks necessary in composing such a work, without having to fight with the software. Clearly, the designers of these software packages have little conception of working with large documents and files and, equally, little interest in addressing the concerns of users. If we allow our large-scale public application with automated biometric identity checks to be designed in the same haphazard and ill-considered manner, we shall certainly experience a far greater number of operational errors than is necessary. This would result in increased operational costs as well as disgruntled users and inefficiency in general. Among currently implemented large-scale systems, there are some good examples of well-considered operational interfaces and some perfectly dreadful examples which are serving no one well. It seems that the importance of this factor is not universally well understood.

What is true for users of our application also rings true for our operational staff. Those involved in the registration process will find their work more enjoyable if the supporting systems are attractively presented, intuitive in operation and reliable in use. This will, once again, inspire confidence and ensure that the individuals concerned are able to operate effectively. This should come as no great surprise as it is a fundamental aspect of human psychology that individuals will function better if they are comfortable with both their tools and their surroundings. Furthermore, if we create the right operational environment for the registration administrators, they, in turn, will respond more enthusiastically and sympathetically with the users being enrolled into the system. Little things, such as the fixing and orientation of the biometric devices, the presentation of the enrolment software, the speed and smoothness of operation and the ease with which exceptions may be handled all play an important part in overall usability. The same applies to all subsequent layers of software relevant to the application. For example, the databases where user details are located need to be maintained, backed up and possibly replicated between several locations. While much of this may be automated, there is still a certain amount of manual administration to be undertaken, even in the configuration of subsequently automated processes, where usability and clarity of operation will prove critical to the ongoing operation. Consequently, principles of good design and usability need to be practised in the creation of software at this level also.

You may ask at this point how we may ensure that usability features heavily throughout our application. With regard to hardware, we must think very carefully about usability and, if required, undertake specific research until we are comfortable that we can accurately specify our requirements, safe in the knowledge that the result will satisfy the usability requirements of the majority. Some suppliers and manufacturers would no doubt rather supply something off the shelf in order to suit their own immediate purpose. The more enlightened suppliers will actually welcome a stringent specification as they will readily appreciate that this is leading them towards a better designed product overall. With regard to operational software, this may sometimes prove a little more challenging as not all application developers have an understanding of usability and why it is important, as can be readily seen in much commercial software today. An application developer may be excellent at solving technical issues and getting the underlying functionality to work but perhaps not so experienced in ergonomic design and principles of presentation. In such a case, teamwork can play dividends. Introducing a specialist in usability and design into the development team can result in a far superior product being created. While this may cost a little more at the development stage, it will pay dividends in increased user acceptance and general operational efficiency. It is a factor that rarely features in contemporary application development, but one which has much relevance to large-scale applications featuring a broad variety of both users and administration staff. In such a scenario, we ignore usability at our peril as shortcomings in this respect will lead directly to impaired performance and operational reliability. It is, in fact, a fundamental requirement and yet, a requirement which remains misunderstood by many.

Implementation Factors

4

We have discussed both technical and human factors and now it is time to turn our attention towards implementation, where we consider what it takes to deliver a fully functional application. Actually, one could write an entire book on this subject alone, so we shall content ourselves with drawing attention to some of the key issues in this context, with a special emphasis upon the operational factors rather than dwelling on technical or infrastructural issues which, in any case, will be application specific.

The inclusion of such a section is considered relevant as it is all too easy to think of applications as just another product to be bought and deployed against a target cost and theoretical benefit model. This is the 'accountants' approach and it is one which may work up to a point, at least for a small, mature application package to be deployed in an equally contained environment with a small number of experienced users. However, for complex large-scale applications, a little more attention is required. For complex large-scale applications which feature automated biometric identity checks, a lot more attention is required. If we fail to understand this point, it is likely that we shall run into a considerable number of operational problems, thus extending our time to reach a state of reliable operation and, in so doing, incurring significant additional cost. Accountants please take note. It is often the areas which we take for granted which have the most potential to be troublesome if we do not pay particular attention to them. We shall therefore highlight some of these issues.

4.1 Training Operational Personnel

We should remember that to many of our administrative and operational personnel, the concept of automated biometric identity checks will be considered as something quite new. While having heard of biometrics, they will have had little or no direct experience with either the technology or the administrative functions necessary to

© Springer-Verlag London 2015

J. Ashbourn, *Practical Biometrics*, DOI 10.1007/978-1-4471-6717-4_4

manage users and support the application. It follows then that they will need some in-depth training in order to understand the various issues around the use of such technology and, specifically, to be able to play their own part in the smooth ongoing running of the application. It is also apparent that these individuals need to be trained and in place at the time of implementation. This means planning in advance and understanding the fine detail of the application and how it will be deployed and operated, well ahead of the implementation date. This is not a huge task providing that a systematic and sensible approach is taken. The BANTAM Program Manager software, which is readily available online, includes modules to help you with such a task, in addition to managing implementation in general, even for multiple sites or projects. It is recommended that you familiarise yourself with this software and make good use of it in relation to your own program.

Having acknowledged that we shall have to train our operational personnel, the question then arises of what this training should consist of. Each application will have its own special needs of course, but we can perhaps make some generalisations. Firstly, they will have to understand the science of biometrics, at least at a high level. They will need to know how biometric technology works, how templates are created, where they are stored, how and why we experience errors, how to use biometric devices properly and how the biometric devices integrate with the host application. They will additionally need to understand the characteristics of the particular biometric devices chosen for this program and how they might differ from other devices as popularly deployed. Depending on how far you want to go, you may also touch upon areas such as vulnerability, security, performance metrics and an in-depth overview of different techniques. All of this may be configured into a specific training package and clearly documented using the BANTAM methodology. This approach promotes reuse and can form the basis of more elaborate training programs, perhaps for commissioning engineers, and can also facilitate multiple language training material as the BANTAM notation is language independent. You should also include a practical 'hands-on' element at this stage, to enable the trainees to use biometric devices themselves and gain some initial familiarity.

After introducing them to the fundamentals of biometric technology and how it applies to our particular application, we must now turn our attention to their own situation and the tasks which they will be required to perform as part of their administrative duties. This might usefully be separated out as a distinct training module and run on a different day to the technology introduction. Perhaps one of the primary tasks for the operational personnel will be to register and enrol users into the application. They must therefore understand not only the precise operational routines associated with this task but also the vagaries of biometric enrolment, including an appreciation of user psychology, and how to deal with exceptions. Hopefully, these individuals will be chosen partly because of their existing people management skills and will be able to clearly explain the process to new users and guide them accordingly. Some of these operational personnel will no doubt be deployed at the day to day points of presence where the automated identity checks are undertaken. These individuals will need to know how to manage exceptions effectively within a real-time operational environment and, importantly, how to quickly distinguish between types of exceptions and the likely reasons for them. They will need a certain level of technical understanding to be able to distinguish between possible technology or system malfunction and user error. In the latter case, they will need to be able to ask the right questions in order to determine why the user is having a problem at that time. They must also of course be able to distinguish between an innocent user error and an impostor attempt. We can appreciate that these individuals will need specific skills in order to properly undertake the various tasks associated with their job. We must therefore clearly identify these skills and create suitable training programs in order to support our operational personnel. We must additionally take great care in designing the associated processes in the first place, ensuring that they are realistic and workable under live operating conditions. We may then configure the various training modules and start planning the overall training program and the logistics of providing this to the right people at the right time. Naturally there will be a cost associated with this activity, but the investment made at this stage will be amply repaid when the application goes live and transactions start to accrue. To look at this another way, imagine a large-scale application with potentially millions of users, where such an investment has not been made. Registration centres may be staffed by individuals who have received nothing but a short instruction on how to use the enrolment software. Operational points of presence are staffed by personnel who have had no instruction other than to divert exceptions to a security area for closer scrutiny. In such a scenario, we would be producing varying qualities of reference biometric templates and users who don't really understand how the system works, because the registration staff didn't understand this themselves. When it comes to live transactions, the error rates will be considerably higher than necessary, causing a disproportionate number of legitimate users to be diverted to another process by staff who do not understand why errors have occurred and cannot explain the situation adequately. Imagine the impact of this spread across multiple operational sites dealing with very large numbers of transactions. A veritable nightmare would no doubt ensue. If we are to avoid such nightmares, then we must take the subject of operational personnel training very seriously indeed. These individuals, and their particular skills and attitudes, will in fact have a direct bearing upon realised application performance. They may be considered as a very important systems component. One which, if malfunctioning, will have an immediate and negative effect upon the application in general. It is recommended therefore that, as a minimum requirement, we configure and provide the following aids for them:

1. An introduction to biometric technology, how it works, how we measure performance, how biometrics are used within broader applications, the importance of human factors in relation to biometrics and an overview of the primary biometric techniques. This module should include a practical hands-on element in order to provide some initial familiarity.
2. An in-depth overview of the host application, why it exists, how it works, why biometric identity checks have been incorporated into it and what the expected benefits of this will be.
3. An in-depth introduction to the registration process, covering the registration routine itself, the perceived variables among human subjects and how to deal

with them, how to create a good quality template, how to test for a good quality template, how to handle exceptions and how to manage security.

4. An in-depth introduction to the real-time operational process and situation including environmental issues, user psychology, understanding possible technical malfunction, dealing with exceptions, dealing with complaints, dealing with possible impostor attempts, falling back on manual processes, associated responsibilities and reporting.

The above-mentioned training modules should be considered in depth and properly documented with example scenarios, systems configurations, process flows, frequently asked questions and a glossary where appropriate. You may additionally wish to provide some accreditation, perhaps in association with an examination or a satisfactory hands-on demonstration. All of this may be managed using the BANTAM Program Manager and its integral tools.

4.2   Training Users

If training operational personnel is important, we may be sure that training users is just as important. A user who feels confident about the technology and how they are going to interface with it is likely to experience fewer operational errors than a user who does not have this advantage. Similarly, a user with a good understanding of both the technology and the host application will more readily understand why an error has occurred and how to manage their way through it. Of course, it is also beneficial if the user has equal confidence in the organisation who implemented the application and their integrity in doing so.

We may consider user training overall in two ways. Firstly, education and secondly, specific training. The education phase is important as we shall need to communicate our intentions to the user base at the appropriate time within the overall project and, later, manage the logistics of inviting them to register into the system and enrol their biometrics. Let's tackle this in a logical order. Firstly, having decided that we are going to implement such an application, or perhaps add the biometric identity check to an existing application, we must communicate with the user base and advise them that we are doing so and why. At this stage, we should provide them with a good background overview of biometrics, how the technology works, why we are suggesting the use of our preferred technique and how it will work in our application, including the usage of their biometric template. If we are seeking feedback from the user base before finalising our application design, then this should be made clear and the appropriate feedback mechanisms provided. If this information is presented in an attractive and truly informative manner, we will have achieved much in warming users towards our project and raising their confidence in the overall management of this application. In this respect, the Biometrics Constitution should be our guide and the Biometrics Charter Document our primary communication vehicle for the prospective users. We should at this stage additionally ensure that an information desk is established in order to make these documents available and answer any associated questions from users. We may also make use of an online portal in order to disseminate such information. The finer logistics of this will of course depend upon the scale of the operation.

Having set the scene and made our intentions clear, we may then proceed to manage the logistics of registration and biometric enrolment. There are various ways of facilitating this according to the use of existing interface channels, antici-pated time scales and a number of other factors. It may be pertinent to provide users with a choice, or indeed multiple choices, and request their response accord-ingly. In any event, this will need to be carefully managed, especially in the case of a large-scale application dealing with a diverse user base. In certain situations, for example, it may be necessary to prepare all relevant material in multiple languages and have similarly equipped information centres available. If, due to user popula-tion size, we are addressing the situation in planned phases, perhaps by user pro-file, geography or some other criterion, then we shall also need to manage this process carefully in order to catch any 'strays' or 'orphans' from our defined groups. For public applications, we may also take advantage of mass media com-munication techniques in order to ensure the most complete coverage of our tar-geted sector. For many large-scale applications, it may be that, before we have had any face-to-face contact with users at all, there is a great deal of communication and education which needs to take place. It makes sense to address this properly, right at square one, ensuring that by the time users present themselves at the regis-tration centre, they have a pretty good idea of what is going on, what is required from themselves and how they are going to be interfacing with the application. They may then concentrate on the registration process itself without distractions or spontaneous emotions clouding the issue.

This brings us on to the training element. We may like to prepare users in advance by providing them with a simple step-by-step overview, perhaps as a handy card or flyer, of the registration and enrolment process. We may also make this information available on the Internet, via our existing offices and other channels, ensuring the best possibility of reasonably informed users presenting themselves at the registra-tion centres. Upon arrival, we may like to check their understanding and answer any additional questions they may have before proceeding with the registration process. It is likely that we shall have required them to bring documentary evidence of their identity, and if they do not have all the required documentation or there is some question as to its authenticity, then we shall have to explain an exception process to them and instruct them accordingly. If all is in order, we may proceed to the biomet-ric enrolment stage, where we should explain the process in detail and preferably give them a chance to undertake a 'dummy run' before actual enrolment. Upon suc-cessful enrolment, they should be given the opportunity to immediately undertake a live transaction or two in order to test the effectiveness of their biometric template and their own understanding of how to interface with the application. This will also serve to build confidence in the process. Finally, they should be presented with a simple flyer which reminds them of how to give a live biometric sample and who to contact if they have any further questions. I can see accountants throwing up their hands in horror at the thought of producing all this material and the extent of the suggested facilitation for users. However, to not do this sufficiently well would, in most cases, almost certainly prove a false economy as we accrue live transactions and encounter errors and misunderstandings which could have been avoided. Taking a little extra care in the initial communication and registration stages will pay dividends for subsequent live operation.

We may like to draw a line at this stage and convince ourselves that we have now attended to user training requirements and can move on to other things. However, user training never really stops as there will always be issues and exceptions which will need to be addressed. Some individuals will forget most everything you have told them and lose the information you provided. Some individuals will feel sure they have understood everything you said but will falter at the first live transaction because, in fact, they have misunderstood the process. Some individuals will experience persistent operational problems and may need to re-enrol their biometric. Individuals below the current usage age will mature and need to be incorporated into the system. Individuals otherwise deemed to be out of scope, perhaps in the context of a voluntary application, may suddenly become within scope. It will be necessary to maintain a constant education and training capability throughout the life of the application. The scale of this facility may vary from time to time and in proportion to the host application, but it will never disappear entirely. It makes sense then to take the subject of user training very seriously and ensure that this area is properly resourced. Some may adopt an alternative view, choosing to wait until the time of actual usage in order to briefly explain the process to users and have them immediately use the system. They may do this with a previously stored reference, on a token such as an identity card or passport, or the biometric may be captured there and then. While such an approach is feasible, it will not result in consistency of use among users, especially for those who are infrequent users of the system. Consequently, each transaction will be taking longer than it needs to, slowing overall throughput and quite possibly introducing unnecessary errors. In short, there is no substitute for proper training and a well-informed user base.

4.3   The Enrolment Process

This section is included because it is considered such an important factor in relation to the successful operation of any application which features automated biometric identity verification. There are some fundamental points to understand in this context. Firstly, and contrary to popular belief, binding an individual to a biometric is no guarantee whatsoever that the individual is actually who he says he is. We are simply aligning a biometric with a described identity which, in most cases, we assume to be correct. This may prove to be a big assumption if an individual has a vested interest in claiming a false identity and seeking to secure it via association with a biometric. Authenticating a claimed identity prior to enrolment thus becomes paramount, especially where eligibility or privilege is associated with identity. Governments seeking to introduce biometrics into national identity tokens or documents would do well to understand the implications of this point. If managed poorly (as, sadly, many such services are), they may in fact be conferring a brace of false identities upon individuals who are criminally inclined. The same individuals may thus access services or claim benefits to which they are not entitled, secure in the knowledge that their biometrics checks against the false identity that they have established, with the help of the relevant government agency. Furthermore, this false identity has now effectively been 'authenticated' by the government, ensuring that these individuals will be considered bona fide and not subjected to undue attention in relation to future transactional processes. If the idea of utilising biometrics in the first place was to be able to have a higher level of confidence as to individual identity, then, in the above scenario, we now have a higher level of confidence, but in relation to a false identity. We would in fact be aiding and abetting the criminal. Viewed in this light, one may readily appreciate just how important the registration process is.

Unfortunately, in many cases of public identity registration, the current authentication process is notably weak and very easily compromised by the determined criminal, many of whom may already have multiple identities. The argument that adding biometrics ensures that the criminal cannot maintain more than one identity is rather tenuous at best. To achieve such a situation would require that every individual coming into contact with the application is enrolled with the same biometric, in the same manner by the same program, with each instance of the biometric enrolled (i.e. two eyes, ten fingers, two hands, etc.) and all of these templates stored within a master database, accessible, in real time, to every application. Furthermore, each individual would need to be checked against each and every template instance at enrolment time and a decision made around likeness to any other instance. Depending upon the biometric technique employed, the match threshold setting and the size of the user base, this may actually prove unworkable in practice. Certainly, we should not base our enrolment process on the assumption that the same individual will not be able to register more than one identity. Consider also the ease with which individuals may enrol into different applications, using different biometrics or alternative instance of the same biometrics, and we can see that multiple identities will not disappear overnight because we have introduced biometric identity checks. Consider also that, for many seeking to circumnavigate the law in this respect, the main task is to establish *any* identity which is acceptable for citizenship and provides the associated entitlements. They only have to do this once. No, if we wish to realise the benefits that biometric identity verification can provide in relation to large-scale applications, we must revisit our identity authentication process (which takes place prior to biometric enrolment) and tighten this up considerably. For some countries, it should be done very considerably. This is another area where operator training is so important.

Given the above observations, we need to consider several key steps as part of the overall registration and enrolment process. The first of these is to identify our user base and communicate the new application process to them, advising clearly on what they need to do to qualify for enrolment and how to apply. There are various ways of undertaking such a task and much may depend upon whether the new process is voluntary or mandatory. If the latter, then we shall probably embark upon some sort of communication campaign. We need to make quite clear what sort of documentary evidence of identity is required and stress that this will be verified against source. We should beware of accepting singular documentary evidence which itself may be fraudulent, such as a passport or driver's licence, and instead insist on several items which, in combination, would be much harder to falsify and which offer additional scope for verification. In addition, we should complement this evidence by introducing associated random checks against place of employment, family connections, other agency records and so on, followed by a short interview with the applicant. This may seem a little draconian but, in the case of a legitimate identity, there is nothing onerous about such a process. Furthermore, it should be stressed that without satisfying these identity authentication checks in full, the applicant will not be enrolled into the system and therefore will not be entitled to any of the associated benefits. It is appreciated that this seems like a hard line to take. However, if we start off with anything even slightly weaker than this as an initial authentication process, we shall simply be creating serious problems for sometime further down the road. Indeed, anything weaker than this would serve to create a golden opportunity for any individual looking for a new identity, for whatever reason, to establish such an identity and have it verified by the state. Of course, this has already occurred and upon a significant scale. The problem is we do not understand that scale as it is likely that the vast majority of such false identities will never be discovered. Some might argue that this is OK, as long as *an* identity has been established and is being used. However, such an assertion would seem to defeat the object of introducing biometrics in the first place. The primary identity authentication process must therefore be as robust as we can reasonably make it. It must also be properly documented and readily available for all to see and understand. A flyer could be introduced for this purpose, outlining the acceptable options and how the applicant may proceed through the process. Legitimate citizens who may have questions or concerns about the process should be able to contact an information point in advance and discuss the situation to their own satisfaction. It may be that the authentication process cannot be adequately completed in one visit, in which case we should consider the options for a suitable process accordingly. Such a robust and well-documented approach may actually serve us well in combating fraud as we may well discover all sorts of interesting inconsistencies, especially with respect to documentary evidence. In this respect, we do of course need a defined and documented process for instances where the operator has serious doubts about the authenticity of the identity being claimed. This may involve reference to other agencies and we must be sure of the associated responsibilities in this context. The operator must also be confident of how to deal with such occurrences and, especially, how to approach and liaise with the individual involved, who may actually be a hardened criminal and may even be regarded as dangerous.

Having satisfied ourselves as to the true identity of the applicant, we may now turn our attention to enrolling the biometric and aligning it with this qualified identity. Depending upon the biometric technique chosen and the specific capture devices being used, we shall have previously evolved and documented a physical enrolment process considered to be efficient and repeatable. We shall have also made decisions around an acceptable matching threshold for our purpose and what constitutes a usable biometric template, i.e. a quality criterion. Providing that our biometric capture devices are calibrated and maintained to a common specification, we may now enrol individuals into the system. We shall probably encounter a small percentage of individuals who have initial difficulty in enrolment and for whom we must provide special attention, maybe over multiple attempts. We shall also encounter a very small percentage of individuals who simply cannot enrol to our required quality standard at all. For these individuals, we must devise an exception procedure and ensure that it is only ever evoked where absolutely necessary. This procedure may involve the use of an alternative biometric technique, more stringent authentication checks or some other process. In any event, the operator must be skilled in identifying genuine exceptions (as opposed to deliberate attempts at non-enrolment) and dealing with them as appropriate. Again, we can appreciate the requirement for highly trained operators. Having enrolled the biometric and aligned it with a specific identity profile, we should check once more that the information is correct and then allow the enrollee to test their live biometrics against the enrolled template in order to verify usability.

One factor we have not yet discussed is the storage of the enrolled biometric template. This may be stored upon a portable token such as a chip card or smart passport. It may be stored within a central or distributed database. Or it may be stored via a combination of these methods, for example on the portable token and also within a database, either as a permanent backup or perhaps temporarily for transactional purposes. We must of course ensure the security of this biometric data and pay particular attention to the various data protection acts in force in the country or countries of use (an application may be operable across national borders). How we choose to store the template will depend upon the application in question and our primary objectives for implementing it. If, for example, our objective is to verify that the holder of a document is indeed the individual to whom it was originally issued, then storing the template securely on the document would seem to make sense. We might additionally choose to store a reference copy of the template within a secure and protected database for backup or emergency usage purposes. If our objective is not associated with the authenticity of tokens or documents but simply requires a biometric identity check at some point within a larger process, then we might consider storing the template only within a database. However, for large-scale applications, such a topography requires careful planning and a robust understanding of systems and network performance issues. With a very large user base, we may well be considering either a distributed or replicated database architecture and this shall have to be properly considered from a number of perspectives including security, data protection, performance, sustainability and business continuity, maintenance and access control. While the enrolment officer may not be too concerned with the finer technical points of such an architecture, they should have a high level understanding of how it works and, of course, the presentation of the software interface at their position needs to be intuitive and unambiguous. Once again, there is a distinction here between closed-loop proprietal applications and large-scale public applications dealing with user bases of national and international proportions.

We have considered aspects of the initial registration and enrolment process, but we should not forget the requirements for subsequent administration. At some point, certain individuals will need to re-enrol their biometrics. When new applicants present themselves, we may wish to check against previously enrolled templates. Or, we may wish to access and search a database for some other purpose. There will be an administrative requirement not only at the registration centres but almost certainly offline as well and we shall have to identify and cater for these requirements in a manner which is in accordance with our principles of security and relative data protection requirements. There is also a maintenance requirement to consider in relation to the registration centres. Firstly, the equipment within them must be set up and calibrated in a like manner against a defined specification. Secondly, this must be periodically checked to ensure ongoing compliance. We do not wish to have individuals enrolled at different centres to a slightly different standard. The use of the Proximity Matching Method goes some way to ameliorating issues resulting from the lack of standards between registration processes and this approach should be considered accordingly. Overall, the registration and enrolment process need not be overcomplex, but it does deserve very careful consideration and definition. If we make mistakes at this point, they may be very difficult, if not impossible, to catch or rectify further downstream.

4.4   The Environment

The operational environment itself is very important in relation to the reliability of biometric identity verification transactions. There are perhaps two elements to this. Firstly, there is the subjective environment from the users' perspective. If the operational environment is attractive and welcoming in its design, then the user will automatically feel better about interfacing with it. Similarly, if it is perceived as comfortable and non-challenging, the user will be more relaxed and likely to give their biometric sample more consistently and more accurately. You may at first consider such matters as relatively trifling compared to the primary technical challenges inherent in such an application. They are in fact very important and can have a direct impact upon operational performance. It is not hard to see the truth of this if you observe the various kiosks which exist in public areas and how people react to them. Take self-service railway ticketing systems for example. If the machines are badly sited, awkward to get at, un-intuitive in their operational logic and unattractive in design, people will mostly prefer to queue at a window to be served by a human being than attempt to use the vacant ticketing machine. Some internal ATM machines in banks have the same problem. In these cases, they do not have to do anything as complex as give a biometric sample, and yet there is a natural resistance to using the automated system. If we now require the user to provide a biometric as well as navigate other functions of the machine, then we had better make the experience pleasurable and intuitive for them. This extends beyond the machinery to the overall transactional environment. This should be clean, comfortable and attractive with sufficient points of presence to avoid unnecessary queues. Much can be achieved with good signage, attractive decors and a logical floor plan which promotes throughput in an unhurried and logical manner.

Making the environment comfortable for the user is, as we have seen, very important. Making the environment comfortable for the equipment is equally important if we are to enjoy reliable operation. Fundamental environmental elements such as light, temperature and humidity are all important to control. Extremes of temperature can affect the operation of electronic subsystems as well as making life uncomfortable for the user. If we are planning to use contact biometrics such as fingerprint or hand readers, temperature extremes can play havoc with the contact surfaces while humidity can similarly affect the optical operation (unless capacitive sensors are used for fingerprints). Equally, with cameras such as might be used with facial or iris recognition systems, extremes of temperature and humidity should be avoided. With facial recognition in particular, lighting is also an issue and we should aim for a consistently lit area without interference from adjacent windows and direct sunlight. If the lighting is too bright and not well diffused, shadows may well affect the efficacy of facial recognition systems. These fundamental environmental issues are obvious when you think about them, and yet some systems have been quite poorly implemented in this respect. In addition to these factors there is the electrical environment to consider. Most electronic devices like to see a clean, smooth, stable power supply of the correct voltage and current, without peaks, troughs, noise or transient spikes. You may be surprised to learn how infrequently this desirable state of affairs actually exists in many modern towns and cities. The consistency of the power grid itself is sometimes quite variable according to usage, and this situation is compounded by the subsystems within major building complexes which are themselves subject to variations. The voltage that your equipment finally sees may be subject to some significant variation, especially at peak loading times. This in itself may not be too much of a problem if the supply is clean. Frequently however, this is not the case and power supplies may be quite 'dirty' with a fair amount of electrical noise and transient spikes which may temporarily inflict high voltages onto circuits which were never designed for them. This is not the ideal diet for our delicate equipment and we would do well to provide main power conditioners and backup supplies for all major items. There is of course a cost involved in doing so, but this should be viewed as a worthwhile investment in the interests of operational reliability. In a similar vein, we should pay particular attention to our system cabling. Skimping on cable specification is not recommended if we are seeking reliable and consistent operation. It is not just the cable either but the way in which it is laid and connected to the equipment. Running data and power cables together in the same conduit or duct may be convenient but will be asking for data corruption related trouble. Using the primary power input cable to the building as a convenient former to which to attach your data cables (as I have seen on more than one occasion) is also not a terribly good idea. Such things are in the realms of installation common sense and yet often get overlooked, especially in multi-tenanted areas where responsibilities are somewhat vague. For our type of application featuring automated biometric identity checks, we have enough operational issues to think about without adding to the complexity with poor quality installations. The operational environment is thus important from several perspectives. In the interests of consistency and reliability, we must strive to provide the best possible environment for both our users and our equipment.

4.5   Installation and Commissioning

Installation and commissioning is an important factor for the implementation of any application, it becomes even more so for applications featuring automated biometric identity checks. We shall concentrate therefore on this element rather than trying to cover every aspect of a typical application. In this respect, let us assume that the underlying network and supporting computer infrastructure has been designed and installed to an acceptable standard. Let us also assume that our particular application is spread across multiple operational sites and will feature multiple registration centers, all of which will be connected via a central administrative hub.

Let us start with the biometric capture devices themselves. They should meet a common specification, even if they have been sourced from more than one supplier. Assuming a multisite operation, it is important that these devices be calibrated within a given tolerance in order to offer closely similar performance. We do not want users to be recognised in one location and rejected in another while providing the same biometric sample. It is also important that the match thresholds are set to an equivalent level in order to provide consistent performance across nodes, unless the Proximity Matching Method is utilised, in which case the issue effectively disappears. If significant numbers of devices are involved, it may be pertinent to test and calibrate them off-site, with a final check and calibration at the time of commissioning. We must also consider the physical installation of these devices. They may, for example, need to be installed within a third-party kiosk which contains other equipment. In such a case, we should ascertain that the power supply is acceptable and that the physical connections are well considered. It should be possible to easily swap out a device for maintenance purposes with the minimum interruption to normal service. This means having standard connectors of good quality for both data and power. In addition, the physical mounting of the device should be both robust and tamper proof and conceived in a manner to support ergonomic operation. If token readers are involved, as would be the case when using chip cards to store the biometric template, then we must consider the reading mechanism and its deployment. We may like to consider a noncontact (RF) token and reader in the interests of read reliability, although we must understand the data security implications of such a design. If we choose contact technology, then the token readers should be robust and as tamper proof as we can make them. In some situations, this may suggest the use of a shutter to cover the receptacle when not in use. There are many variations on a theme when it comes to using tokens and we shall not cover them in depth here but recommend that security of installation, perceived usage and MTBF (mean time before failure) requirements and read reliability are all taken into careful consideration with whatever technology is chosen. Finally, we should ensure that the biometric capture device and associated token reader where applicable are not

subject to either physical or electrical interference from other elements of the installation. It goes without saying that we should have also considered the security of
data passing to and from these components and the relative vulnerability to attack.
All of these factors should be taken into account for document readers, such as those
used for reading passports, whether functioning optically or reading from an integral chip in a near-field RF manner.

Associated with the biometric device will be some sort of user interface. This
will include a display with which to provide information and possibly a means for
the user to select options. This may take the form of a 'touch screen' display within
a kiosk, or perhaps a display and set of multi-action buttons, depending upon to
what degree the user is required to interact with the system. However simple or
sophisticated this interface, we should ensure that it is robustly installed and capable
of withstanding the expected usage. We should also ensure that it is easily accessible for maintenance purposes and that the various components may be easily and
quickly exchanged. The precise location of any such kiosk or visible user interface
may be important in areas where natural light is present. Clearly we would not want
the screen to be in direct sunlight, making it difficult for users to see what is being
displayed. Small points such as this can make a big difference in terms of reliable
operation. For the kiosk itself, we shall also need to provide adequate airflow and
ventilation without compromising the physical security of the enclosure. Similarly,
we shall need to provide robust and secure connectivity for both power and data to
the kiosks.

I use the term 'kiosk' to identify the equipment enclosure at the operational point
of presence. Whichever term you adopt, this enclosure will also incorporate some
sort of data processing capability as well as data communication functionality. This
may take the form of a conventional computer motherboard with integral LAN connectivity or perhaps with wireless communications capability. It will be important
to ensure that these devices are properly and securely mounted and that they are not
vulnerable to electrical interference or physical attack. We have already mentioned
the importance of power supplies and ventilation in relation to the installation of
such equipment, and it follows that, in the interests of reliability, we need to provide
a stable operating environment for the equipment within these kiosks. If the location
itself is subject to environmental extremes, then this may mean providing thermo-
statically controlled cooling or heating in order to maintain operational equilibrium.
We have also spoken about the siting and specification of cables. The kiosk is a case
in point. We should ensure that all data and power cables are secure within robust
conduit and routed in such a way as to inhibit electrical interference. This may be
difficult within a shared operational environment due to the topography of other
cabling and available ducts. However, we should persevere with this cause and not
accept compromises which may leave us vulnerable to either environmental interference or attack. This is an important point, as all our efforts in providing a reliable
and secure kiosk may be rendered superfluous if the data is interfered with, intentionally or otherwise, beyond this point. In this respect, we should consider the
system as a whole, even if comprised of disparate components, including cabling,
physical connections, power supplies and everything else that goes to make up the

complete installation. This should also include components which are dependent upon our application. For example, it may be that as a result of a validated biometric check, a turnstile or barrier is activated to grant passage to the user. In such a case, this equipment should also come under our scrutiny, with the same principles applied to vulnerability and operational reliability.

We have so far focused upon the operational side of the application, but we must be equally vigilant with the installation of equipment at the administration positions, including the registration centres and any central data processing facility. In each case, we must be conscious of vulnerability, reliability and operational security, planning our installation accordingly. This is not especially difficult, but it does require a certain commitment to these principles and a willingness to invest properly in them. Here lies a potential problem. It is fashionable these days to outsource factors such as installation and commissioning. You may find this acceptable for a small application of little significance. For a large-scale application, especially one in the public domain, we should think very carefully about taking such a step. If it is unavoidable due to lack of in-house resource or capability, then we should issue a very precise specification and ensure, by careful audit, that it is met or exceeded in every detail. On no account should the management of installation and commissioning be handled by a third party in respect to an application of this type. The agency responsible for implementing such an application must take proper responsibility for its correct installation, just as they must do for communication with potential users of the system.

When it comes to commissioning the installed system, this should be undertaken according to a carefully prepared script which ensures that every element is thoroughly checked for both operation and performance. In fact, it may be pertinent to have a series of such scripts to cover the primary operational components at different locations. Use of the BANTAM methodology can be especially helpful in this respect, as suitable scripts may be constructed from the same system architecture maps used in the application development, ensuring that every detail is adequately covered. The same material may be reused again for training purposes. Having prepared suitable scripts, the commissioning engineer may systematically work through them, adjusting or correcting as he goes and finally certifying each operational area as fit for live operation. It will be important though to understand the concept of true end-to-end performance and ensure that a final test is undertaken from this perspective, that is, after testing each sub-assembly and individual component, testing the whole application in relation to that specific location, including data communications, database performance where applicable, interfaces and data feeds to and from other systems and local exception handling routines. This may be time consuming but will be worthwhile in identifying any overlooked details or incorrect assumptions (there will always be some). Finally, the commissioning engineer should produce a detailed report, confirming his tests and, if applicable, certifying that particular location as fully operational. If it is not possible to do this, then a fault rectification summary should be produced and issued to management. When such faults have been properly attended to, the commissioning may be undertaken again and certification finally granted. All this may sound a little like a military campaign, but it is so important to get things right at the outset, especially with applications featuring automated biometric identity checks, where external factors can have a significant impact upon realised performance. Such attention to detail will be amply rewarded in the longer term.

4.6 Technical Support

Having discussed installation and commissioning, we must not forget the requirement for ongoing maintenance and support. Getting the system up and running is one thing. Keeping it that way is just as important. Furthermore, we shall want to gather statistics about performance, including the performance of the biometric identity check, and possibly fine-tune certain system parameters as we learn from operational experience. It follows then that we shall need to establish a technical support capability, both to maintain the system, support administration staff where necessary and to monitor overall systems performance. These are important tasks which require knowledgeable and responsible individuals to undertake them. Ideally, these individuals should be sourced internally and trained specifically in the support of this application. We should not assume that existing IT support personnel will have a sufficient understanding to be able to maintain or comment upon the operation of the biometric functionality. In all probability, this will represent a new challenge for them and they shall have to be trained specifically in this area. If it is anticipated that technical support for this application will be subcontracted, then this will have to be managed very carefully by the implementing organisation. We shall not wish to find ourselves in the position of training engineers 'on the job' who have not had previous exposure to this type of application. It may well be that we establish experts in certain areas of technical support, for example, those expert in data communications, biometric verification technology, database management, user support and so on. We must also understand the requirements according to scale, ensuring that sufficient coverage is provided across all areas for both typical operation and exceptional circumstances. This will mean having the right number of trained individuals on hand at the right locations to cover every eventuality.

You may reasonably ask who trains the technical support staff with regard to the biometric functionality and any other unusual aspects of the application? Do not assume that the necessary information can be simply picked up from the supplier literature or website. Technical support training requirements need to be considered right at the start of application development. If the application design has been well documented, using BANTAM, for example, then this will easily be managed by reusing many of the specific BANTAM maps and building a training program around them. The BANTAM Program Manager software makes the management of this task even easier with the provision of schedules and associated course management. It will probably be appropriate to divide the training requirements into distinct modules, thereby facilitating specialisation as well as providing training in easily managed chunks. In this respect, a senior support engineer may decide to take every module, while a specific area specialist will just take those most appropriate to their area. It is important to tailor the training precisely to the application in question, ensuring that technical support personnel fully understand the systems architecture and associated functionality. It is acknowledged that many will have existing general skills and technical expertise, but we must ensure that they understand the specifics of this particular application and operation. This means also understanding the jobs and processes of those personnel at the operational sites, registration centres and central administration areas and being able to advise them on systems- or process-related matters. Indeed, they should be able to slot into any one of these positions seamlessly if required. It goes without saying that they must be able to quickly identify systems or component malfunction and be able to rectify such a situation without undue delay. Support staff must also have a solid understanding of information technology in general, including communications, data management and infrastructural design. Naturally, you will have an inventory of essential spares in order to facilitate such a response.

A related area within this broader context is management reporting. Part of the application design process will have identified the required management reports from this application. These may include transactional throughput, overall systems availability and performance, error rates associated with the biometric check and a variety of other parameters. The technical support personnel must understand how these reports work, where the primary data is coming from and how to troubleshoot them when things go wrong. They should also be capable of running audits and checking data accuracy in relation to any such report. This may be no mean task in the case of a large-scale multisite application with, perhaps, a central reporting function. In such a case, there may be several linked databases and perhaps a data warehouse or data mart against which reporting is run. All of this will need to be understood by the technical support team. A log management system should also be in place in order to identify lower-level systems-related issues as well as providing an audit trail. Systems such as the innovative APEX mechanism for automated control provide communications and transaction monitoring at a high level, together with basic reporting and centralised management. Such a system would represent a good starting point for any multi-node application.

We have simply glanced upon a few obvious points in the above dialogue and yet, it may already be appreciated that the technical support function is an important one which needs to be properly planned and resourced. It is not enough to simply sign an outsource contract and hope for the best. We must look at this area very carefully if we are to maintain an efficient and reliable operation over time. Furthermore, it is likely that an application such as that discussed will be handling personal data which is subject to local data protection legislation. We shall have to ensure not only that we are compliant with any such legislation but that we can readily demonstrate such a compliance. This requires a strong in-house technical understanding and a properly documented application design. This in turn requires the establishment of a competent technical support facility.

In conclusion, we have discussed, within the last three chapters, various aspects associated with the implementation of applications featuring an automated biometric identity check. We have emphasised the importance of understanding the special requirements of large-scale applications, such as those within a public domain, and drawn attention to some of the associated technical and human factors. You may wonder why an application featuring biometrics is any different to any other application. In order to understand this distinction, we might usefully analyse the underlying functions. Essentially, we are binding an individual to a defined identity via biometrics and then measuring them against this biometric reference in order to satisfy ourselves as to their identity in relation to the provision of some service or other. We are automating the biometric identity check and therefore making an entitlement decision based upon the functioning of a technical apparatus and associated software. If this check is in anyway flawed, we shall be making the wrong decision and either denying an entitled individual, or perhaps worse, allowing a non-entitled individual access to the service. We must therefore be extremely sure of our application and its operational integrity. In order to arrive at a suitable level of confidence, we must fully understand all the variables likely to affect the reliability and integrity of our operation. This is why we need to pay particular attention to human factors as well as technical factors and implementation issues. We have discussed these briefly within these pages and the prospective implementing organisation or agency is encouraged to take this thinking further via practical experience gained via small-scale trials and relevant technology testing. The remainder of this book examines various utilities which will aid the understanding of pertinent factors in this context. The BANTAM Program Manager software application will also be discussed before moving on to consider future scenarios and the longer-term implications of the widespread deployment of biometric identity verification technology.

Associated Utilities

5

There are a number of software utilities, freely available from the Biometrics Research website, which serve to demonstrate some of the fundamental factors associated with biometric identity verification technology. These may be used for educational and training purposes and will prove especially useful for those involved in application design at both the broader and more technical levels. In particular, these utilities serve to aid the questioning of certain assumptions which have prevailed for a long time in relation to the efficacy of biometric technology. A more complete understanding of such assumptions and the underlying technical factors associated with them will help in the conception and design of more robust systems. An overview of some of these utilities is provided herein for the same purpose. It is recommended that the reader studies this section carefully and takes time to absorb the principles discussed.

5.1 The Biometric Performance Simulator

The rationale behind the Biometric Performance Simulator was to demonstrate the principle of equivalence of performance across operational nodes or points of presence. The simulator employs a subset of the APEX technology which was developed to effect an equivalence of realised performance across nodes, via an active feedback mechanism. In such a manner, any number of operational nodes may be controlled from a central management position, with confidence that realised operational performance would be essentially equivalent across nodes and maintained accordingly. The APEX software allowed for a database of operational nodes and secure communication between each node and the central host. This allowed for a chosen level of realised performance to be set centrally and instantly communicated to every node on the system. Individual nodes would then self-adjust to the new performance criterion, reporting the results back to the central management position. The APEX system also allowed for exceptions to be raised as alerts and for a

© Springer-Verlag London 2015
J. Ashbourn, *Practical Biometrics*, DOI 10.1007/978-1-4471-6717-4_5

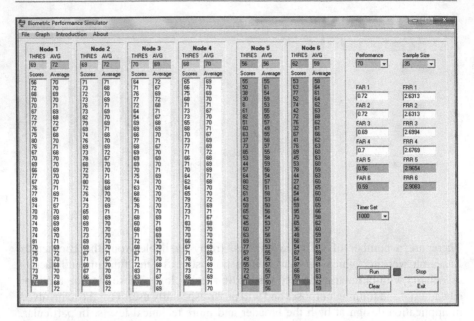

Fig. 5.1 The main BPS interface

full audit trail of realised performance to be maintained. Consequently, it could be demonstrated that, at any given point in time, all the operational nodes (points of presence) on the system were performing to an equivalent degree with regard to biometric matching performance. Users could thus have confidence that their biometric matching transaction would be undertaken to an equivalent degree, anywhere on the system and without prejudice as a result of ill-considered configuration. Similarly, the operating agency could have confidence that every operational node within the broader system was performing to an equivalent standard, thus enforcing an operational rigour throughout the entire system. Furthermore, the level of performance being realised would be defined and recorded. This approach offered the additional benefit of being able to raise or lower the desired performance (and thus matching accuracy) across the entire system according to prevailing conditions. Such a brace of capabilities significantly exceeds the common practice of having fixed matching thresholds, configured independently at every operational node. The Biometric Performance Simulator allows for the primary concept to be clearly demonstrated by simulating collections of random transactions at a number of nodes, four of which are being managed by the innovative APEX system, while two behave in the conventional manner.

The Biometric Performance Simulator is shown in Fig. 5.1 having just been run. The panel at the right-hand side contains two boxes at the top which allow performance and sample size to be set. The performance criterion is based upon a scale of 1–100 and is aligned with the potential matching performance of the biometric devices employed throughout the system. The sample size relates to the number of sampled transactions within a set, which itself serves as a performance indicator for monitoring purposes. To use the wizard, one simply selects a performance level, a sample size and a timer interval and then clicks on the Run button towards the bottom of the panel. The simulator will then generate six sets of random transactional data, emulating six nodes or points of operational presence. At the interval set by the timer (which is scaled in milliseconds), these six sets of transactions will be generated, according to sample size, and displayed in the left-hand column of each node. Upon every occurrence, the average of these transactions will be calculated and this figure added to the right-hand column for each node. Subsequent iterations of the process will generate further average figures to be added to the right-hand column until either the wizard is stopped (by clicking on the Stop button) or the column becomes full, in which case the wizard automatically stops. Throughout this process, one may observe the results in the boxes above the node columns and within the right-hand panel. For each node, there is a threshold setting and an average box, the contents of which change with each set of samples. The average box shows how closely the transactional performance is aligning with the desired performance criterion, and the threshold box shows how the matching threshold is being automatically adjusted after each sample set, in order to realise the desired performance. As we can see in this example, the four APEX controlled nodes are maintaining a level of realised performance extremely close to that set at the desired level, while the uncontrolled nodes are failing to do so. In the right-hand panel, for each sample set, a false acceptance rate and a false rejection rate are calculated for each node, illustrating the relationship between these factors and overall performance. In the menu bar, one may click on the graph command in order to plot the entire series graphically.

From Fig. 5.2 we may readily understand the distinction between the APEX controlled nodes and the conventional nodes. The realised performance of the controlled nodes is very tightly grouped and consistent across multiple sample sets (36 in this instance, i.e. $36 \times 35 = 1,260$ transactions per node). However, the two uncontrolled nodes have failed to realise the desired performance. Furthermore, their performance has been considerably more erratic with wider swings between the extremes. If, in this example, all six nodes had been uncontrolled, one might imagine what this graph may have looked like and the wide variance across nodes from the desired systems performance. Now imagine that there are 250 nodes, and one can begin to appreciate why equivalence of realised performance across operational nodes is important. Now let us imagine that events have conspired which cause us to desire an increased level of performance for a period of time. With the APEX methodology, we can simply select the new level of desired performance and download it instantly to every node on the system. Every point of presence will then automatically adjust itself to this new level of performance.

We have now increased the level of desired performance to a figure of 80, as depicted within Fig. 5.3. As before, we can readily observe that the four controlled nodes have quickly acclimatised themselves to this new instruction and have attained a performance level extremely close to that desired. The uncontrolled nodes however, with no connection to centralised management, cannot respond to this new

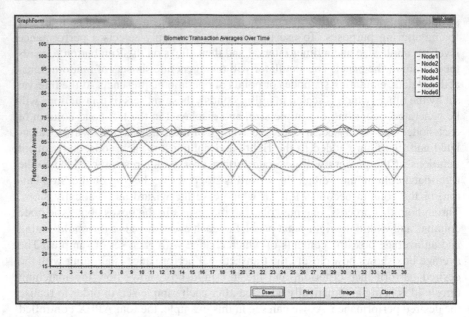

Fig. 5.2 Plotting the transaction series

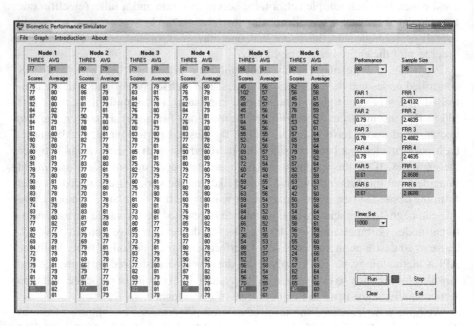

Fig. 5.3 Increasing the desired performance level

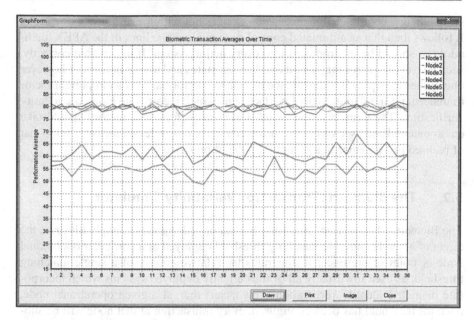

Fig. 5.4 The uncontrolled nodes are even further from the desired performance

requirement. In order to change their level of realised performance, a commissioning engineer must go and physically alter the configuration parameters at each node. If one has 250 nodes on the system, this will take quite some considerable time. Furthermore, the probability that each of these nodes will be configured to realise a similar level of performance will be extremely low indeed. After a few such operations, the reality will generally be that every node on the system will be performing quite differently. This, in turn, means that users will have a different experience at every node and that, in some cases, substantial error rates will be experienced. This chaotic situation shall, of course, be quickly exploited by those who have reason to do so, seriously negating the value of the system in overall terms.

In Fig. 5.4 we can see that, as before, the performance of the controlled nodes is grouped very tightly and maintained at the desired level, as set from the centralised management position. The uncontrolled nodes are now performing at a level which is hopelessly adrift of that required. Furthermore, their individual performance remains erratic and error prone.

The purpose of the Biometric Performance Simulator is to illustrate that, if uncontrolled, disparate operational nodes will be delivering realised performance in a completely uncoordinated manner. Furthermore, over time, the disparity will simply increase as local engineers tinker with threshold adjustments in response to variations of perceived local conditions. The result is that the operating agency will actually have no idea of how the system is performing overall. More worrying perhaps is that they will also have no effective control over overall systems performance. In exceptional situations, they will simply not be able to adjust the overall system in any coordinated manner and certainly not within a responsive timescale. It follows then that an automated control system, along the lines of the APEX methodology, should be incorporated into every major system. If undertaken correctly, such a level of control may be attained across states and across borders or however one wishes to deploy it. Equivalence of realised performance is an important factor to understand in relation to deployed systems which incorporate biometric identity verification. The term 'realised' is used as such performance metrics should take environmental and user variations into account, the only relevant measure being that of realised performance at a particular point of presence.

5.2   The Biometric Transaction Variability Simulator

The Biometric Transaction Variability Simulator is designed to simply illustrate the effect of a single, variable matching threshold deployed at a particular operational node or point of presence. It illustrates the relative crudity of a single matching threshold, as used in virtually all of the currently deployed systems which incorporate biometric identity verification. This means that, at a given operational node, once the threshold has been configured, every transaction at that node will be subject to the same matching criteria, regardless of individual template quality and regardless of the myriad of human factors which make every transaction subtly different. Imagine that once a particular operational node has been configured and activated by the commissioning engineer, a thousand individuals pass through this node every day, males and females of differing ages, differing ethnicities, differing states of health and differing levels of experience with the system. The combination of reference template quality and human factors will ensure that, wherever the matching threshold is set, it will be inappropriate for many individuals, possibly even for the majority of individuals passing through that particular node. Consequently, the confidence that we may entertain towards the result of the matching transaction is compromised. Unfortunately, not many seem to understand this point and prefer to assume that the result of the biometric match may always be relied upon. Such a confidence is misplaced, especially when, in the majority of cases, the operating agency has little idea of where the matching threshold has been set and why. They assume that if a positive result is obtained, then the individual must be who they claim to be. Such an assumption is very heavily flawed. In addition, depending upon precisely where the threshold is set, they may be experiencing a significant number of false positives, of which they will be blissfully unaware. In other words, individuals who have a notion to do so may be routinely defeating the system, and the operators will not even realise that this is occurring. The Biometric Transaction Variability Simulator provides a graphical representation of the implications of deploying a single matching threshold for all transactions at a particular operational node. Bear in mind when using this utility that you may effectively multiply the inherent uncertainties of this method by the number of nodes deployed across the system. In which case, it may safely be assumed that the operating agency in question actually has no idea at all of the matching accuracy being realised across

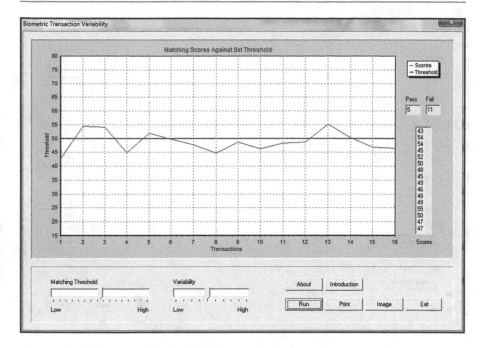

Fig. 5.5 A typical standard threshold setting

the system, and for all users. Similarly, with respect to automated systems, it will have no idea how many false positives are occurring and, therefore, how many individuals are effectively defeating the system. Bearing in mind that a false positive may be a correct biometrics with incorrect credentials as well as the other way around. The author drew attention to this reality more than a decade ago, but the point remains misunderstood by many operators.

Biometric capture devices and their attendant software will be preconfigured with a standard threshold setting, designed to offer a reasonable level of performance in terms of error rates. However, the supplier has no knowledge of the special circumstances of specific implementations. Usually, the matching threshold may be adjusted on site in order to alleviate perceived problematic operation, although such a facility may be a mixed blessing, as will be apparent when using this utility. In Fig. 5.5 the threshold has been set at a standard setting of 50, which the supplier believes will result in equal error rates (i.e. an equal probability of false negatives and false positives). We have simulated a batch of 16 random matches, the scores from which are shown within the right-hand column. Note that we can alter the variability of these transactions although, in this case, we have assumed a median setting. Of our 16 transactions, 11 have failed, which we assume as false negatives. In other words, 11 out of 16 valid users have been rejected by the system. This could be for a number of reasons. Nevertheless, from the user's perspective, they have simply been rejected by the system in error. In such a situation, the operator, perturbed by the difficulty being experienced by users, will almost certainly instruct the

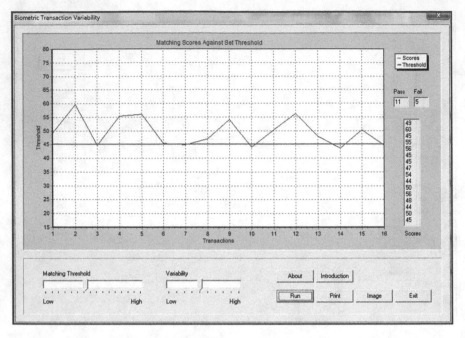

Fig. 5.6 A slightly reduced threshold setting

technical support team to adjust the system for 'better' performance. They will respond by reducing the matching threshold level in order to reduce the number of realised false negatives.

The results of this reduced threshold setting, from 50 to 45, may be seen in Fig. 5.6. Another batch of 16 transactions is run and, this time, there are only 5 false negatives, a more satisfactory result from both the user's and operator's perspective. However, how many false positives have occurred? We simply don't know as there is no way, in an automated system, of telling. It may be that all 11 of the other transactions are correct, or it may be that two or three of them are actually false positives, directly enabled by the reduced threshold setting. When large numbers of transactions are being undertaken at a given operational node, a false rejection rate of just 1 or 2 % would be unfortunate. When this rate becomes around 20 % or more, it will probably be considered unacceptable and the threshold setting will no doubt be reduced in order to realise a lower error rate. This weakening of matching accuracy would seem to defeat the object of employing biometrics and automation in the first place, and yet, this is exactly what happens with respect to many automated systems. In such systems, it is only false negatives which are readily apparent and, in our efforts to reduce these errors, we shall be increasing the probability of realising false positives, although we shall not know when these have occurred. Later in this chapter, a methodology for vastly improving on this situation will be introduced. When using the utility, experimentation with the Variability slider, even at a constant threshold setting, will demonstrate the effects of user and environmental variability, both of which can be significant within the context of a particular system.

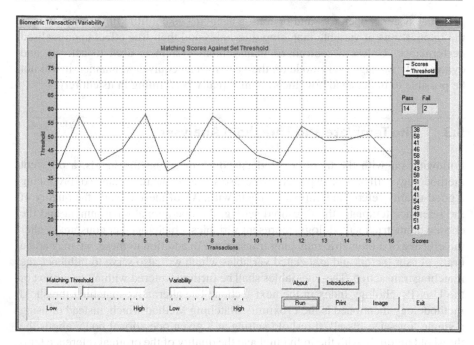

Fig. 5.7   Reducing the threshold even further

In Fig. 5.7 the matching threshold has been further reduced in order to realise a more acceptable false-negative error rate. In this example, 2 out of 16 transactions have resulted in failure and this still represents a significant error rate. However, of the 14 transactions deemed to have passed, notice the wide variability of scores, which themselves represent a degree of likeness between the reference biometrics and the supplied live sample. Within this variation, it is quite possible that a number of false positives may exist. The threshold could be further reduced to a point where realised false negatives are negligible. However, this would mean that almost any-one could present a biometrics to align with a claimed identity and be accepted by the system. As previously stressed, the operating agency would, in an automated system, have absolutely no idea that such false positives are occurring although, in effect, they would be positively inviting them by manipulating the single matching threshold per node in this manner. If, within a multi-node system, the majority of nodes had been subjected to such manipulation, with no coordination between them, which is often the case, then the actual realised performance of the system will be unknown. Furthermore, the realised performance variation across nodes will also be unknown. However, those with a will to defeat the system will no doubt quickly identify nodes which have been subject to such threshold manipulation in order to reduce the occurrence of false-negative errors and will exploit the situation accord-ingly. The same principles apply wherever biometrics are used to verify personal identity in relation to the provision of benefit, whether for crossing a border, making a payment, receiving state benefits or some other application. It is important that potential systems operators and operating agencies take a little time to understand the implications of variable matching thresholds and their true effect upon realised performance. Unless a centralised management system is used to actively and dynamically manage every node on the system in an equivalent manner, it will not be possible to understand how the system is really performing in its entirety.

5.3   The Template and Threshold Analyser

Following on with the theme of understanding matching thresholds, a different methodology will now be explored while also stressing the importance of producing a good-quality reference template to begin with. All of these factors, the quality of the reference template, the threshold setting, the operational environment and the chosen biometric methodology, represent variables which together conspire to alter the efficacy of a biometric matching transaction. In addition to these, we may add a brace of user factors and associated variables which will also serve to influence the matching transaction. These variables shall be further explored within the context of the User Psychology Index in the next section. The alternative matching threshold methodology mentioned is the Proximity Matching Method which, instead of using a single 'one-size-fits-all' threshold setting at a given operational node, aligns the threshold uniquely with the individual and the quality of the original reference template. This approach introduces the dual benefits of increased matching accuracy and reduced errors. It achieves this as, in effect, it is asking a completely different question at the time of matching. Rather than asking 'is this provided sample likened to the reference to the degree set by a fixed threshold?', it asks, 'is the provided sample likened to the reference with a certain plus or minus tolerance, according to the quality of the individual reference template?' In such a manner, a broad range of user-related variables may automatically be catered for without compromising the threshold setting for other users. In addition, such an approach recognises the variables introduced by the ageing process as the user updates his or her reference template. Within systems which constantly refine the reference template, this is an automatic process which tracks the shifting situation automatically, ensuring that the matching transaction is pertinent and always falls within the prescribed limits. Furthermore, the Proximity Matching Method allows for adjustment, not by arbitrarily moving a fixed threshold back and forth but by increasing or decreasing the tolerance level either side of the nominal according to the quality of the reference template. It is an altogether better approach, the details of which have been made freely available to all by the author in the interests of the common good. It will be interesting to see to what extent the Proximity Matching Method will be adopted by the biometric supplier industry. The Template and Threshold Analyser wizard clearly demonstrates the distinction between the two approaches discussed while allowing pertinent factors to be adjusted, in order to gauge their effect upon the results of the matching transaction.

The wizard allows the random variation of template quality, a single matching threshold, environmental variation and tolerance in respect of the Proximity

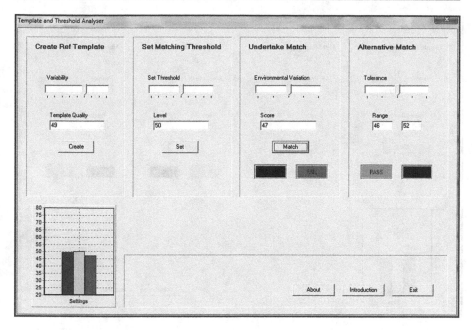

Fig. 5.8 An average case

Matching Method, referred to here as an 'Alternative Match'. Figure 5.8 depicts a scenario whereby the random template generation process has achieved a quality score of 49. The matching threshold has been set at a median point of 50 and the tolerance level has also been set at a median point, based directly upon the quality of the original template. In this case, the Alternative Match is seeking a transaction likeness score of between 46 and 52 based upon a reference quality of 49. Clicking on the 'Match' button undertakes the transaction, introducing its own level of randomness based upon environmental conditions, as happens in reality. In this instance, the matching transaction has returned a likeness score of 47, quite close to the original reference template. The conventional fixed single threshold system has rejected this transaction, simply because the score did not pass the arbitrarily set threshold, even though it was very closely matched to the original. This has resulted in a false negative. The Alternative Match process however has recognised the true likeness to the original as the score falls neatly within its tolerance levels and has quite correctly recognised this as a perfectly valid transaction. Note that using the Alternative Match process will be different (and more accurate) for each individual as the tolerance will be directly linked to the quality of the reference template. In Fig. 5.8, the graph in the left corner shows how closely these factors are aligned and yet, the conventional system has generated an error due to the unsuitability of an arbitrary single fixed threshold at a given operational node. It is curious to reflect that this obvious weakness has remained unaddressed by the biometric industry for so long, resulting in deployed systems which are, at best, compromised with respect

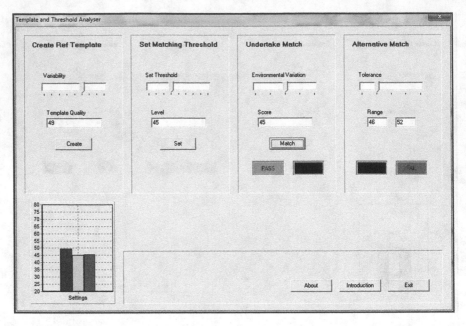

Fig. 5.9 A case of manipulated thresholds

to their operational efficacy, especially where large numbers of users are registered into the system. As the user population grows and, to a proportional degree, ages, the errors will tend to increase, resulting no doubt in further manipulation of the single threshold settings employed.

In Fig. 5.9 the same reference template is employed, but this time, the single fixed threshold has been reduced to a setting of 45 in order to alleviate instances of false negatives. Indeed, when a subsequent transaction is undertaken, a score of 45 is produced, and, as this is just within the limits of the adjusted threshold, the transaction has been passed although, actually, this represents a false positive. The Alternative Match process however has deemed that this score lies outside of the agreed tolerance, based upon the original reference, and has failed the transaction accordingly. This example serves to illustrate how false positives may unwittingly be introduced by reducing a single fixed threshold in order to counteract instances of false negatives, a practice which is common with respect to deployed systems. The graph illustrates that the single threshold and resulting score do not reflect the quality of the original reference template. While this may be deemed a borderline case, there may be a very large number of such transactions within a large deployed system operating across a number of operational nodes or points of presence. Consequently, in real terms, matching errors occurring within such a system may be much higher than is supposed. Variations of the single fixed threshold across nodes simply serve to exacerbate the issue.

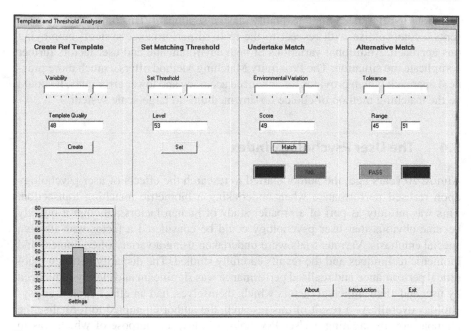

Fig. 5.10 Another example

The example portrayed in Fig. 5.10 depicts a slightly different situation. In this case, while potential template variability has been increased, this particular template has nevertheless delivered a quality level of 48, which may be considered as average. In this example, the single matching threshold has been increased to a level of 53, perhaps in an effort to improve matching accuracy. Environmental variation is slightly higher than average at this node and, in this particular instance, the matching process has returned a score of 49 which, actually, is very well aligned with the reference template. However, on this occasion, the single fixed threshold system has failed the transaction as the score did not reach the arbitrarily set threshold level of 53. The Alternative Match system set its tolerance level, based upon the reference template, to between 45 and 51 and, consequently, regarded the transaction, quite correctly, as a pass. This example thus depicts a situation whereby the user has provided their live biometrics in a very precise manner, achieving an extremely close likeness to the original reference template. This transaction should clearly have been regarded as a successful pass, and yet, the system employing the single fixed threshold has failed the transaction, thus creating a false-negative error. The system employing the alternative Proximity Matching Method has recognised the high degree of likeness to the original reference template and has, correctly, regarded the transaction as a successful match. This wizard enables a wide range of scenarios to be established with the implications upon realised performance displayed quite clearly. It demonstrates that a single fixed matching threshold is a disingenuous way of attempting to match biometrics from a wide range of individuals, among which variations in reference template quality may be significant. This immediately represents a compromise with respect to the realised performance systems employing this approach. Additional variations of both environmental and user factors further complicate the situation. The Proximity Matching Method offers a much more practical approach which provides for enhanced accuracy and lower error rates. It should be the matching method of choice for any medium- to large-scale system.

5.4   The User Psychology Index

Almost 20 years ago, the author started to research the effects of user psychology upon realised performance when undertaking a biometric matching transaction. This was initially as part of a broader study of human factors although it quickly became obvious that user psychology could be considered a factor with its own special emphasis. Various trials were undertaken using a variety of equipment and biometric techniques and the results carefully studied. The disparity between theoretical performance and realised performance was significant and clearly influenced by user and environmental factors which, themselves, had an effect upon user psychology overall. As a result of this research, the author attempted to formalise the phenomenon by creating a User Psychology Index, the purpose of which was to devise weightings that could be added to theoretical performance figures in order to align them more closely with real-world deployments of the technology. This index was further aligned with the Biometric Operability Index which sought to create a further alignment between biometric techniques.

The User Psychology Index was subsequently refined and translated into a simple software wizard in order that various scenarios could be explored and their effects upon probable performance noted. This wizard was included with various software applications but is now available as a simple stand-alone utility. It is particularly useful for educational purposes as it enables students of biometric technology to create various scenarios for discussion purposes and, if necessary, to debate the findings, perhaps in relation to different biometric techniques. It further encourages the simulation of these scenarios within a test environment, with real devices and actual translations. When used in this manner, the User Psychology Index can be a powerful and inspirational tool, leading to an enhanced understanding of user factors and the effect of user psychology upon realised performance. This intelligence, in turn, may inform the precise configuration of systems parameters, allowing a system to be attuned to its operational environment and user base. Consequently, the User Psychology Index wizard should be a part of every systems integrator's toolkit and could usefully be studied by every implementing agency. The use of the wizard is explained as follows (Fig. 5.11).

When starting the User Psychology Index wizard, the user is presented with a tabbed dialogue with the first tab (Device Details) selected. Navigation between tabs must be undertaken with the buttons at the bottom right of the screen as these also serve to save the results of each section. On each screen, the user will find a clear explanation of the parameter under discussion and, with the exception of the

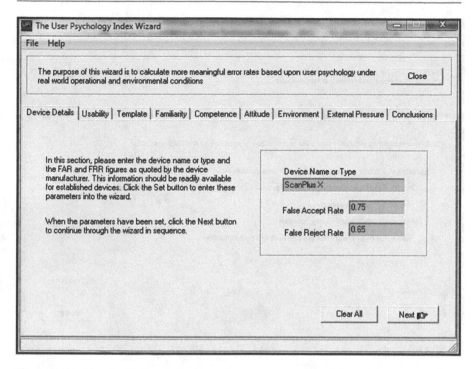

Fig. 5.11 The User Psychology Index first page

first screen, simply has to select a value from a drop-down dialogue box. Operation
of the wizard is thus extremely straightforward. On the Device Details page, the
user may enter a descriptive name for the device under consideration (often the
manufacturer and model name) and the published performance values for both the
false acceptance and false rejection rates (sometimes referred to as false positives
and false negatives). These are the metrics typically published by device manufacturers to describe the theoretical performance of their particular device or software.
How these figures are arrived has often fuelled controversy. Sometimes they are
extrapolations of theoretical performance derived from algorithm matching statistics, sometimes they are based upon offline tests undertaken against known databases of reference biometrics and sometimes they seem to exist with little foundation
at all. In the vast majority of cases, they will not be based upon real-world implementations of the technology in question, hence the requirement for such a wizard.
Other possible metrics will be discussed later (Fig. 5.12).

The Usability page is concerned with usability of the biometric device in context.
This includes the user interface, the associated software, how well the user is guided
through the process and, of course, the perceived operability and performance of the
device and any associated hardware, such as a turnstile, for example. There are
many factors to consider in this respect, including the operational environment. Is it
a comfortable and welcoming environment with clear, unambiguous signage? Are
user variations well catered for, for example, individuals who are taller or shorter

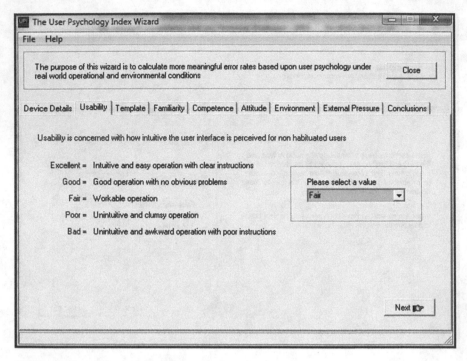

Fig. 5.12 The usability section of the wizard

than average, individuals who have physical disabilities, individuals who are poorly sighted or hard of hearing? These exceptions may appear obvious, but there are less obvious user-related conditions to consider, such as those who may have learning difficulties or other idiosyncrasies that render interaction with the system more difficult than it is for others. If no assisted usage is in place, instances of exceptions such as those described will result in higher-than-expected error rates, particularly in relation to infrequent users. Much may be achieved by an intelligently designed, welcoming environment wherein users feel relaxed and able to concentrate on the process at hand. It is interesting to note how poor many public-facing systems are in this respect, with ill-considered placement, poor signage, inadequate lighting and little attention paid to throughput. The wizard allows a value to be selected from the drop-down box on the right-hand side of the form, with explanations of the available ratings on the left-hand side. This is the common interface for other parameters within the wizard (Fig. 5.13).

The importance of template quality has been discussed and readers will readily understand that a poor-quality reference template will prove troublesome in subsequent matching transactions. This, in turn, will prove frustrating for users as they struggle to match their live sample with an inadequate reference. Naturally, this will result in operational errors and shall thus affect the realised performance of the system overall. The same holds true even for non-live, offline matches where one stored biometrics is matched with another or against a database in a one-to-many

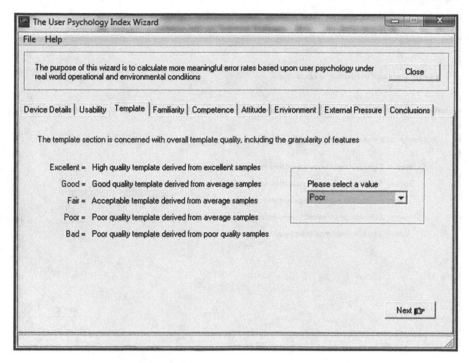

Fig. 5.13 Template quality

match. Poor-quality reference templates constrain the efficacy with which a biometric matching transaction may be undertaken. While most enrolment software provide a quality check of some description, variations will still occur as a product of individual physical characteristics. Furthermore, software utilised at enrolment stations will typically be configured differently in this respect, allowing a further degree of variation. Multiple reference templates matched against a single threshold setting will likely result in variations of matching accuracy, as a product of varying template quality. User psychology becomes a factor, both at the time of enrolment and in relation to subsequent matching transactions, and this reality should be taken into careful consideration when designing systems, including both the operational software and the physical environment of enrolment stations (Fig. 5.14).

Many users of systems incorporating biometric identity verification will be infrequent participants, for example, when exposed to automated border controls at a country that they hardly visit or in relation to a process with which they rarely need to interface. They may remember that they need to provide a biometrics, but the probability is that they do not remember the idiosyncrasies of the particular system involved. Furthermore, even if the system is similar in concept to another with which they are more familiar, for example, one using the same biometrics, it may be configured in an entirely different manner. Consequently, for a great many users, the process of interacting with the system and providing their biometrics will be one of limited familiarity. The probability that they will seamlessly flow through the

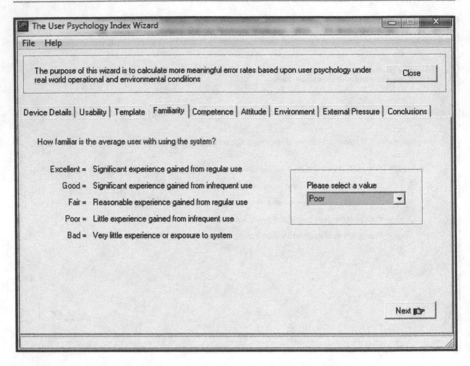

Fig. 5.14 Familiarity

process without a hitch is accordingly reduced. For first-time users at a particular point of presence, the process may seem completely alien, depending upon where and when they registered their reference biometrics and what they remember of the instruction given at the time. We may conclude that, within a given user base, there will be variations of familiarity which shall have a direct effect upon error rates and overall systems performance. As such systems become prevalent, there will be an attendant issue as a result of a lack of equivalence of both performance and process between systems. For infrequent users, this will serve to confuse them even further, especially when things don't work quite as expected at a less familiar site. Many of these issues may be ameliorated, at least to some degree, by good-quality guidance and training (Fig. 5.15).

It may seem strange to include a section on competence, but it is an important factor with respect to overall systems performance. Within an application which features biometric identity verification, the user effectively becomes a systems component. Consequently, the efficacy with which that component functions has a direct effect upon the broader application and its realised performance. Competency is one of many user variables and is itself directly linked to user psychology. It is possible that even a frequent user, with familiarity of a particular application, may be more or less competent with regard to the interaction with technology and the consistency with which a live biometrics is supplied. Some will have a keen interest in the technology and will strive to understand how best to use it. Others may have little or no

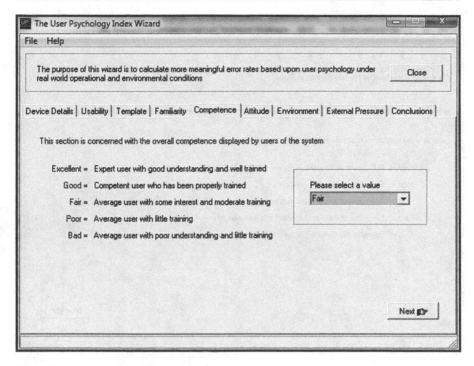

Fig. 5.15 Competence

interest in technology and will simply expect it to work, without taking the time to understand how or why. The former will be able to understand errors in context and will probably be able to extricate themselves from exceptional situations and failures. The latter will struggle to do so. The solution is, of course, to ensure that all users are properly trained and that, where required, documentation is available with which to describe the application, how it works and how best to interface with it. For all such applications, a Biometrics Charter document should have been produced and this will serve as a first step in this context. The Biometrics Charter may then be complemented by a simple step-by-step user guide to be made available upon request to all users. Without these aids to user competence, the natural variability within a large user base will, together with other human factors, conspire to affect realised performance with respect to individual matching transactions and, therefore, the system overall (Fig. 5.16).

One of the most important factors within the broader concept of user psychology is undoubtedly attitude. Individuals will have different views about the use of biometric technology and why they should be compelled to participate in related applications. Some will see the use of biometrics as an invasion of personal privacy and will worry about the use of their biometrics, where it is stored, who might have access to it and why and how it is managed over time. Others may not be concerned about privacy and will perceive the application of biometrics to everyday transactions as a positive step. Some may adopt a philosophical view, either that the

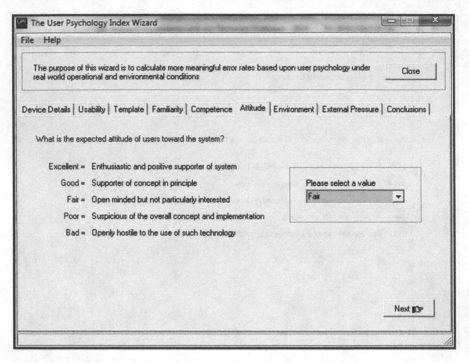

Fig. 5.16 Attitude

widespread use of biometrics is inevitable or perhaps that such developments are ultimately against the interests of the common good and should not be tolerated. Some may consider that the widespread adoption of such techniques by government agencies has nothing whatsoever to do with security (as they claim) but is purely a means to exercise increasing levels of control over ordinary citizens. Whatever stance an individual adopts on the subject, it is likely that their perception will be strongly defined. This perception and attitude, both towards the technology in principle and to its practical implementation, will undoubtedly influence the manner in which the individual interacts with the system and hence with the implementing agency. From a systems perspective, it is likely that those with a negative perception will be less consistent in their use of the system than those who believe such systems to be a good thing. Interestingly, this attitude can change, and in either direction. Individuals may become more or less in sympathy with the concept as their knowledge of what is really happening develops. Thus, the effect upon realised performance may also change over time (Fig. 5.17).

It is curious that, in relation to deployed applications, the operational environment seems rarely to receive much consideration. Deploying agencies may argue that this is because applications are often deployed in shared environments (e.g. airports), where they have little choice in such matters. However, even in shared environments, much can be achieved with a little thought and forward planning. Furthermore, it is important to do so, as the operational environment can exert a

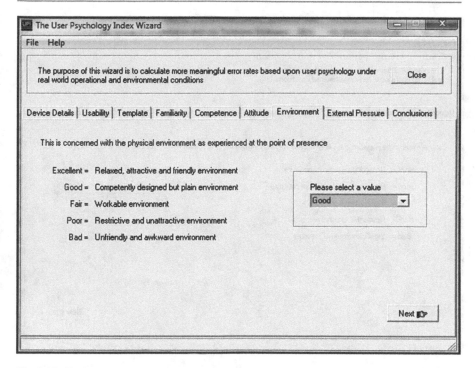

Fig. 5.17 Environment

strong influence upon users, for better or for worse. A poorly conceived operational environment will generally make an equally poor impression upon users which, in turn, will influence the way they interact with the system. The opposite is also true, in that a well-considered, attractive and efficient environment encourages users to interact positively with the system, resulting in fewer errors. Simple factors such as clear signage and instructions can make a significant difference in this respect, as can an intuitive user interface and maintaining sufficient points of presence to maintain throughput without unnecessary congestion. Non-application-specific factors such as a comfortable temperature and even illumination are also important, as they serve to create a welcoming environment. Many operating agencies will scoff at such suggestions, claiming that users simply have to do as they are told. This attitude is unfortunately prevalent in many countries and it is an attitude that ultimately serves no one well. A little extra consideration and respect for users can go a very long way in terms of maintaining an efficient operation. An operating agency (whether governmental or commercial) that understands this point will typically enjoy an application with fewer errors than the norm as users will be much more positive about the application and the agency responsible for it (Fig. 5.18).

Individuals maintain a unique blend of physical and nonphysical characteristics. Often, the two work together, particularly in response to encountered situations. There is an additional variation in the manner in which individuals respond to unexpected situations or those which place them under pressure. Some individuals are

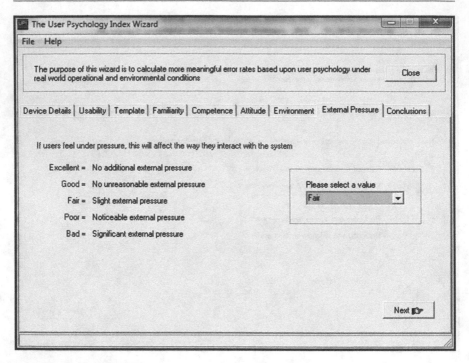

Fig. 5.18 External pressure

ebullient and take everything in their stride. Others are more introvert and are inclined towards shyness within a public situation. However, all will feel pressurised, to a greater or lesser degree, in certain situations. Imagine, for example, an individual who is already late for an important appointment and is rushing to get through an automated control point where there is already a queue. Having waited for their turn, the individual then fumbles the act of providing their biometrics and is failed by the system. Frustrated, and perhaps a little annoyed, they try again, very quickly, and are once more refused. Depending upon their precise character, the user may now be feeling very self-conscious, especially if a queue is forming behind them. This emotional stress may also result in a physiological response. Hands and fingers may sweat, pupils may become dilated, facial expressions may change and so on, resulting in further complications with respect to the biometric matching transaction. The combination of these factors will certainly affect both the manner with which the live biometrics is presented and the likelihood of a match against the stored reference. Consequently, errors will occur which would not have occurred under a less stressful situation. External pressure is therefore a factor which will affect the realised performance of a given system. The design of the operational environment, the operational process and the systems interface should take this into consideration.

In this example, we have chosen a mixed set of values, from poor to good, for the various parameters of the wizard, as may be seen in Fig. 5.19. The left-hand

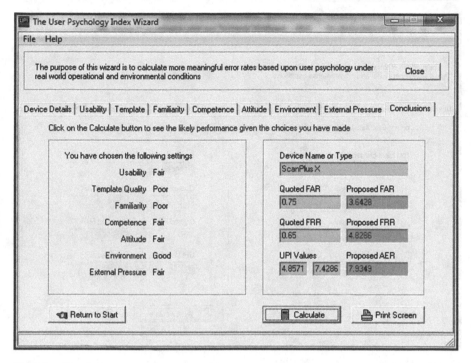

Fig. 5.19 Conclusions

pane of the wizard confirms the values chosen for each parameter, and the right-hand pane shows the results of our theoretical scenario when we click the Calculate button. The quoted false accept and false reject figures are shown and, in the green boxes to the right, proposed values are shown, based upon the choices made. Note the magnitude of the disparity. And yet, these figures, as proposed, are not unusual in real-world applications. A new metric is introduced here, a proposed average error rate. This single figure is derived from the other metrics and provides an easier way of understanding the magnitude of likely errors while also making it easier to compare the results of different scenarios as configured within the wizard. The Print Screen button is self-explanatory and allows for the results of each configured scenario to be printed out for subsequent analysis. The example given within Fig. 5.19 may be said to represent a typical implementation and serves to illustrate that theoretical performance figures, as might be quoted by a device or systems supplier, are rarely realised under real-world operational conditions. The disparity between the two will depend upon how well the supplier has estimated the performance of the system in question. Even when matching algorithms have been tested against known databases of static images, this is no guarantee that similar results will prevail in live systems. There are simply too many variables involved to be able to predict this accurately. The User Psychology Index wizard can help to predict a more likely performance under real-world operational conditions.

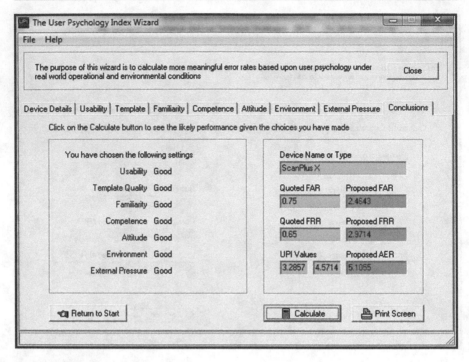

Fig. 5.20 Different conclusions

Figure 5.19 illustrated what might well be a very typical, real-world scenario. Some might argue that their particular application and user base is rather more positively attuned to real operations. In Fig. 5.20, a more positive scenario is configured with 'Good' chosen for all parameters (there is also an 'Excellent' weighting that may be applied). Even with all parameters configured as 'Good', we can see that the wizard has suggested a significant departure from the quoted figures, with a proposed average error rate of 5.1 %. This may not seem like too high a figure in practice; however, depending upon the number of users involved, such an error rate may cause significant operational issues. If, in response to the magnitude of such issues, matching thresholds are reduced, then the system overall will not be performing as intended and will, at best, represent a compromise in terms of identity verification. The User Psychology Index and the associated wizard illustrate the importance of user factors and user psychology in relation to the realised performance of a given system. Such factors should, of course, be considered at the design stage of a given application and should be reflected in the functional design, the operational process and the configured environment. This would seem an obvious point to stress and yet, it is surprising how many applications are very poorly considered in this context. There seems to be an assumption that a (live) biometric match is a reliable, consistent process, unaffected by external variables. This is simply not the case, at least not when dealing with users submitting a live biometrics for comparison with a stored reference. There are some applications of course when there is no live biometrics involved as a previously captured biometrics is simply compared against a database in order to find a match. Such systems are subject to a different set of variables, mostly associated with the quality of the biometrics involved. Of course, even in the context of these systems, the original biometrics were captured from users in some sort of live environment and so, user factors and user psychology remain relevant, albeit in a slightly different way.

5.5   Conclusions

Within this chapter, various utilities have been explored which, together, enable a more enlightened perspective to be developed with respect to the use of biometrics for identity verification purposes. Having read this chapter and, hopefully, experimented with the utilities described, it will be appreciated that factors such as biometric matching thresholds and associated algorithms, the equivalence of realised performance across operational nodes and user psychology, play a very important part in the performance and general efficacy of applications deploying biometric technology. It is important therefore for systems designers and operating agencies alike to take the time to really understand these factors and ensure that the design and implementation of the application is sympathetic towards them. Unfortunately, in the rush to implement such systems, this has rarely been the case. Too much emphasis has been placed upon theoretical performance and assumptions based upon supplier-generated information and not enough on proper analysis of the application at hand and its real objectives. Consequently, there are a number of poorly implemented applications, some of them of quite a high profile, currently in operation. However, they may be improved. It is never too late to revisit the situation and, if required, to reconfigure the system, revise the operational environment and develop a better operational process. The utilities referred to in this chapter are all freely available from the Biometrics Research website and are self-explanatory as to their use, although guidance is also provided within each utility. They may be used effectively by technical designers, application developers, operational personnel and even politicians. Their use will ensure a better understanding of this technology which should then result in better designed and implemented systems.

Using the BANTAM Program Manager

6

This chapter is concerned with the use of an innovative software utility for managing all aspects of programs which feature biometric identity verification and related technologies and which use the BANTAM methodology for defining and documenting the various aspects of such programs and projects. The software is called the BANTAM Program Manager and is designed to run on Microsoft Windows-based computers. The program is not meant to replace dedicated project management software, especially where this is integrated into organisational practice, but to offer a broader high-level view and tracking capability which may be used by managers who are nonspecialist in the use of such software, with very little learning curve involved. Alternatively, it may be used as a dedicated application with which to manage a series of applications which feature biometric technology. In addition, the software has certain capabilities which are simply unavailable in other packages, making it unique in scope.

The BANTAM Program Manager may be used effectively in relation to a single project, but its real strength lies in managing multiple projects within an overall program of works. This might be the case, for example, where you have an application deployed across multiple physical sites, each one of which requires its own local project management and might have purchase orders and invoices raised in relation to it. In addition to managing the high-level definition of such multiple projects, the BANTAM Program Manager also acts as a document management system, making it easy to find a particular document. Furthermore, such documents may be viewed and edited from within the program, keeping everything neatly in one place. An integral report generator can provide you with lists of documents, personnel and other information on a project-by-project basis, with just a couple of mouse clicks.

The BANTAM Program Manager even extends into areas of training via the creation of training schedules and modules within schedules. To these you may assign individuals and book dates for attendance at particular sessions, maintaining a simple log of who has been trained for what. This in turn makes it easier to assign suitable individuals for specific projects. Add to this functionality fully featured

© Springer-Verlag London 2015
J. Ashbourn, *Practical Biometrics*, DOI 10.1007/978-1-4471-6717-4_6

Fig. 6.1 The BANTAM Program Manager main screen

personnel and supplier databases and one may appreciate just what a useful utility the BANTAM Program Manager really is. Notwithstanding this flexibility and powerful functionality, the program is quite intuitive and logical in use, requiring no special skills on the part of the user. Indeed, typical users will soon familiarise themselves with the program and be enjoying the benefits of being easily able to maintain a high-level view of a complete program of works, no matter how many individual projects it might contain or how many regional offices and personnel are involved. This is the essence of the BANTAM Program Manager (Fig. 6.1).

In this chapter, we shall explore the primary modules and features of the program and explain their use accordingly. However, the user will gain the most valuable insight into the program and its possibilities in relation to their own particular situation, by experimenting with the various modules and features contained therein. In addition, the typical user will want to explore the BANTAM methodology itself and practise the creation of the associated documents using the BANTAM graphical notation. This is a powerful methodology which is well suited to the definition and development of complex or large-scale applications, while remaining intuitive in use for systems developers and integrators, suppliers, managers and everyone involved with such a project.

Using the BANTAM methodology and the BANTAM Program Manager together provides for a simple, intuitive and yet very powerful approach to organising and tracking a biometric program, no matter how complex or large in scale. Furthermore, this approach provides for an unparalleled audit trail, in as much detail as you wish, and for every aspect of your program. It is also very relevant for training purposes and subsequent systems management, as every aspect of the application, including operational processes, will be fully documented and collated within one software program. The ongoing value of such a methodology cannot be overstated.

6.1   Using the Project Manager

The BANTAM Program Manager consists of several modules, an important one being the Project Manager. This is where you define, at high level, the various projects which together make up your overall program. You may select the Project Manager either from the appropriate button on the main toolbar or from the GoTo drop-down menu from the menu bar. Each of the BANTAM Program Manager modules may be selected in a similar fashion and you may switch from one to the other randomly as required. Each module, together with the standard toolbar and menu bar, features its own additional controls as necessary to support its own particular functionality.

The Project Manager consists of two main sections, the Project Definition section and the Resource Allocation section. These work together in order to define your project and allocate human resources to it. You may define multiple projects within your overall program using the Project Manager module and produce reports associated with various aspects of a specific project using the Report Manager which we shall be looking at later on. Before using this module, it will be helpful if you enter a few records into the Personnel Manager database, which you will find an overview of in Sect. 6.4. If you just wish to experiment with the BANTAM Program Manager for now, it is suggested that you enter around 10–20 records in the Personnel Manager. Remember to fill in all the fields for each record as appropriate.

The first step is to give your project a meaningful name. Click on the Insert Record button within the navigation controls at the bottom of the screen (the plus symbol) and type a descriptive name in the Project Name field. You will notice that the Project Number field is non-editable, as the project number is automatically assigned and maintained by the program. Next, select a Project Manager from the drop-down list. This list is populated from the Personnel Manager database, which is why we needed to place some names there beforehand. Note that while the Project Manager field shows just the last name, the drop-down list shows the full name, including middle initial. This helps to distinguish between individuals having the same family name. In the Department field, enter the department in which the project manager is based. You may now assign your own internal reference for this particular project in whichever format you choose. Enter the reference in the Project Reference field accordingly. Lastly, enter a start date and end date for this project using the calendar controls accessed via the arrow to the right of the Date fields. These dates are, at this stage, usually estimates according to your best guest as to the scope of the project. However, this is fine as it establishes a baseline for your project as well as an audit trail of the original thinking around implementation

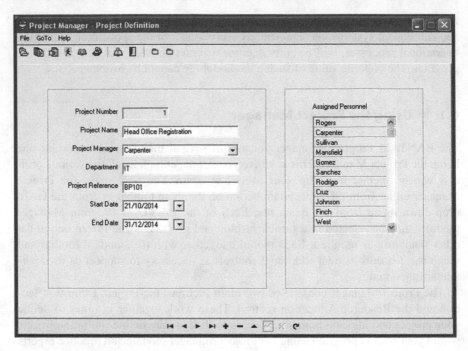

Fig. 6.2 The Project Manager Project Definition screen

requirements. When you are happy with the details entered for this project, please click on the Post Edit button (the check mark) within the navigation controls, in order to save this information as a record in the Project Manager database. The other buttons in this navigation set allow you to move back and forth between records, edit or delete an individual record and refresh the on-screen data.

You have now established a high-level account of one of the projects within your overall program. You may effectively enter as many projects as you like in this way (hundreds of thousands anyway) and, of course, you may edit or delete an individual project if you wish. However, be advised that you should not attempt to delete a project for which documents have been assigned as this would result in orphaned documents. We shall discuss document management a little later on. You will notice in Fig. 6.2 that, in addition to the high-level project details, there is a section of the screen which shows a list of personnel assigned to each project. This list is read only and you cannot edit it from this screen. As you will have by now surmised, this task is undertaken in the Resource Allocation section. On the main toolbar, you will notice two small folder icons. Hover your mouse temporarily over each of these and you will see pop-up descriptions to show that one of them is to select the Project Definition section and the other to select the Resource Allocation section, the two of which together make up the Project Manager module. You may confirm which section you are in by looking at the standard Windows title bar, where the relevant name will be displayed. If you try to select the same section again, an information dialogue will be displayed to remind you of exactly where you are (Fig. 6.3).

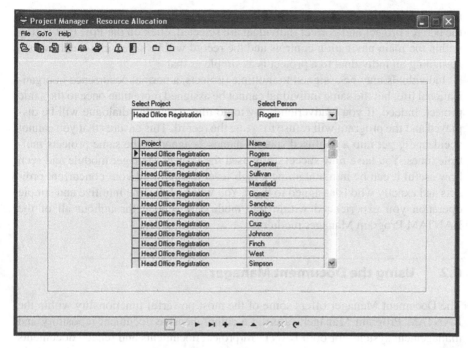

Fig. 6.3 The Resource Allocation section

Let us move to the Resource Allocation page where we shall find a list of projects and individual names assigned to them. Each project and individual assignment is listed on one line as a database record. Hence, you will find the project name mentioned several times, according to how many individuals are assigned to the project. With a large complement of personnel and many projects running at once, this section might start to contain a large number of records. You may move between them easily by using the navigation controls at the bottom of the screen or simply by using the scroll bar to the right of the window in order to view a particular group of records.

The process of assigning an individual is simple enough, but first you must have at least one project defined and a selection of individuals registered into the Personnel Manager database. You may just as easily delete an individual record in order to de-assign an individual from a specific project. The two drop-down list boxes in the top section of the page and the navigation controls situated at the bottom of the page are the tools you use to make assignments. First, select a project from the left-hand list box. You will notice that the record cursor on the left-hand side of the main window changes from a right-pointing arrow to a cursor indicator. This shows that the database is in edit mode and that a record is about to be created. If you happen to change your mind at this stage, you may simply click on the Cancel Edit button in order to return the database to normal mode.

With a project selected in the Select Project list box, we may now select a name from the Select Person list box. You will notice that, although only the family name is entered in the project list, the full name including the middle initial is shown in the drop-down list, ensuring correct selection of the intended individual. When both the correct project and correct individual are selected, click on the Post Edit button within the main navigation controls and the record will be saved into the database. Assigning an individual to a project is as simple as that.

Individuals may be assigned to multiple projects, a normal occurrence in organisational life, but the same individual cannot be assigned more than once to the same project. Indeed, if you inadvertently try to do this, a warning dialogue will be displayed and the program will refuse to create the record. This ensures that you cannot accidentally get into a confused state of names assigned to the same projects multiple times. You have now successfully used the Project Manager module and seen how useful it can be in maintaining a high-level listing of all your concurrent projects and exactly who is assigned to them. You will find that the intuitive and simple operation you experienced within this module is echoed throughout all of the BANTAM Program Manager modules.

6.2   Using the Document Manager

The Document Manager offers some of the most powerful functionality within the BANTAM Program Manager, offering a comprehensive document repository and management system, for both BANTAM project documents and related documents such as purchase orders and invoices. Furthermore, it is easy to associate these documents with projects, authors and external suppliers where appropriate. The Document Manager even allows you to open and edit such documents within its own interface via proven OLE technology. This means that entire projects, including supplier management, purchasing and invoicing, may be managed within one easy-to-use, efficient utility. Using the BANTAM document types and the BANTAM symbol notation, every aspect of any number of projects may be fully documented and then easily referenced whenever necessary, keeping everything in one place. This greatly facilitates auditing, as well as ongoing management (Fig. 6.4).

The Document Manager is divided into three related sections. The BANTAM Documents section, the Purchase Orders section and the Invoices section. Collating all of your purchase orders and invoices associated with specific projects can be extremely helpful, especially in relation to a large program where you may have several projects running concurrently. The Document Manager allows you to achieve this in an intuitive manner and integrates with the Report Manager in order to produce fast reports by project, totalling the values of both purchase orders and invoices. We shall explain this functionality in greater detail in Sect. 6.3.

Let's start by seeing what is involved with entering a BANTAM document into the Document Manager. The first step is to initiate a new record by clicking on the Insert Record button within the navigation group at the bottom of the screen. You will notice that the document is given a unique number automatically and that this is shown in the Document Number field at the top of the page. We should now select the project with which this document is associated from the Project drop-down list box, in which all your registered projects will appear. In the next field, enter a

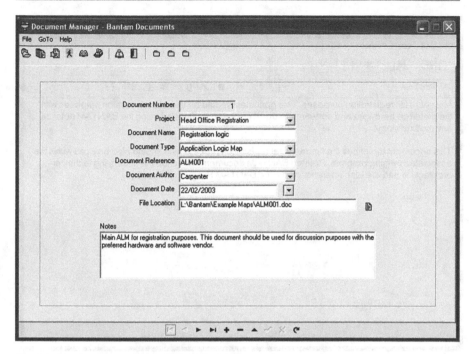

Fig. 6.4   The Document Manager main interface

descriptive name for this particular document. This name should be chosen so as to remind you of the document's contents.

As this section of the Document Manager is dealing with BANTAM documents, we should now choose a document type from the drop-down list associated with this field. All of the standard BANTAM document types are listed here for your convenience. The next step is to select the document author, and, once again, this is made easy by the provision of a drop-down list showing all the individuals listed in the Personnel Manager. It is of course important to note who the document author is in order to understand who is doing what within the context of each project and also who you need to talk to if you have any questions about this particular document. While it is true that their name probably appears on the document, it is not particularly convenient to have to open each document in order to ascertain who authored it. The Document Manager approach is much more intuitive and useful, especially when integrated with the Report Manager. In a similar vein, it is often useful to be able to see at a glance the creation date of a specific document, without necessarily having to open it. Entering this date into the record is easily achieved via the calendar control. Simply click on the arrow adjacent to the Date field in order to open up the calendar control. When you select a date from the calendar, it will automatically be entered into the Document Date field in the correct data format.

Another interesting feature which is to be found in several of the BANTAM Program Manager sections is a dedicated text processor. This may be invoked by

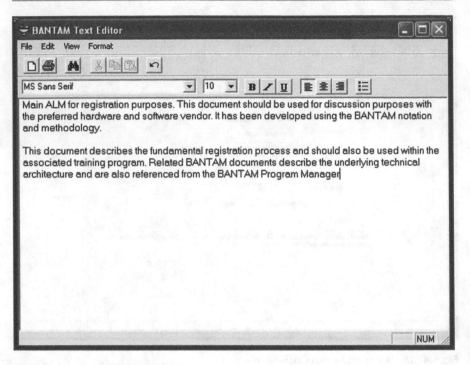

Fig. 6.5   The BANTAM text editor

right-clicking in any of the Notes fields and choosing the Edit option. The text processor is a light word processor which allows for full text formatting and other pagination, including the insertion of bulleted lists and the usual cut, copy and paste functions. While injecting the resulting text into the Notes field when you select Save and Exit from the menu, the text may also be saved as a separate document, a feature which may prove useful if you need to send this information to someone else. Furthermore, existing documents may be loaded into the text editor and subsequently saved into the Notes field in the appropriate BANTAM section. This represents quite powerful functionality which may prove extremely useful in relation to practical project management (Fig. 6.5).

The next field will no doubt prove extremely useful to most users of this software. In the File Location field, enter the precise location on your PC or network where this file is stored. In many cases, different types of documents will be stored in different locations on your network, depending upon who is most frequently accessing them. For example, purchase orders and invoices will probably reside on the accounts department network space. Even BANTAM documents might be filed in different locations depending upon who created them. You may decide upon a separate network location for each project or different folders for different types of BANTAM document or some other unique file storage strategy according to your own preferences. Finding all the files relating to a specific project can therefore quite often be problematic. This often leads to significant duplication as documents

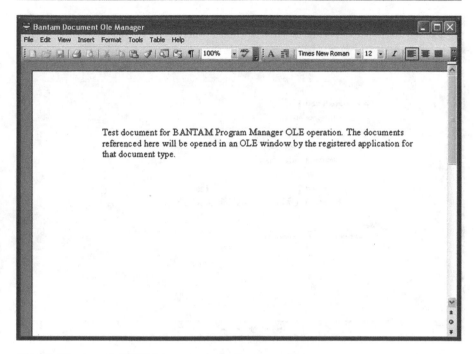

Fig. 6.6 Viewing a BANTAM document in the Document Manager

are copied and stored in multiple locations for convenience. The problem with this approach is of course version control, as the particular document you have accessed might be one or more versions out of date, but you do not necessarily know this to be the case. A much better strategy is therefore to leave the documents where they are and point towards them from a central repository such as the Document Manager. Now, to the right of the File Location field you will find a little document icon. If you click on this icon, you will be able to view the document referenced within the File Location field (Fig. 6.6).

When viewing a document in this way, the Document Manager interface changes to the OLE Manager and the toolbar changes to that of the program required to view and edit the document in question. For example, in the case of a BANTAM document file with a .doc extension, the toolbar will become the toolbar of your local Microsoft Word program, provided of course that you have Microsoft Word installed on your computer. A document file with the .xls extension will display the toolbar from your Microsoft Excel program and so on. This is quite a powerful feature which you will no doubt find useful when using the Document Manager to survey the documents associated with your projects. In the lower section of the Document Manager interface, you will find a Notes field. You may regard this as a free-form text notepad where you may enter notes and observations about this particular document (using the text editor if you choose to). This can be very useful in instances where you have questions about the document which will need to be addressed at a

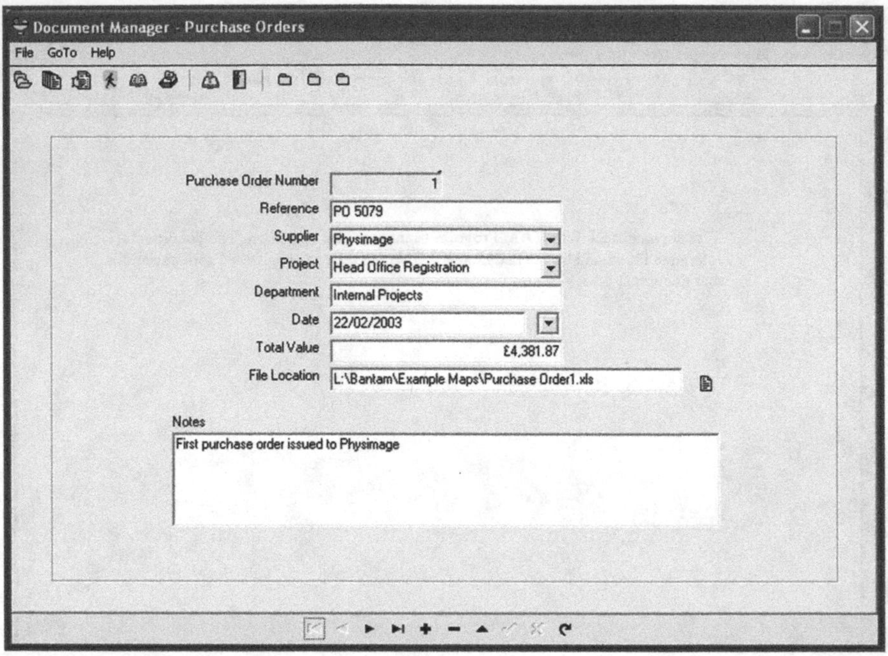

Fig. 6.7 The Purchase Orders section

later date and you do not wish to forget them. When we have completed all the fields
for a particular record, we may click on the Post Edit button in order to save this
record into the database. Let us now go to the Purchase Orders section by clicking
the middle folder icon in the main toolbar (Fig. 6.7).

The Purchase Orders section of the Document Manager operates on similar principles but with a slightly different set of data fields. After initiating a new record,
place an appropriate reference in the Reference field. This would typically be your
own purchase order reference number. Next, select a supplier from the drop-down
list box, which contains all the suppliers within the Supplier Manager database. The
next field is the Project field, for which you should select the project to which this
purchase order pertains from the drop-down list box. In the Department field, you
will probably wish to reference the department who initiated the purchase order
and, in the Date field, the date on which the purchase order was raised. The Total
Value field should of course reflect the total value of this particular purchase order.
The File Location field works in exactly the same way as it did in the BANTAM
Documents section. Enter the precise file location in this field and you will always
be able to go straight to this document.

Once again, this can prove extremely useful, especially when you have a query
from the supplier and you need to quickly check the details of a specific purchase
order. Finally, the Notes field in this section enables the creation of free-form
notes as required in relation to this particular purchase order. Remember to click

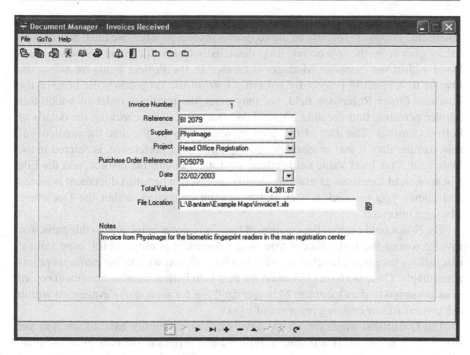

Fig. 6.8   The Invoices Received section

on the Post Edit button in order to save the record. Having this repository of purchase orders at your fingertips can prove invaluable when managing large programs. It can potentially save a good deal of time which might otherwise have been spent running back and forth to the accounts department in order to check the details of a specific purchase order. It is also extremely valuable from the perspective of having a quick check on capital expenditure in relation to a specific project, especially where multiple projects are involved. We can perhaps now begin to appreciate how the BANTAM Program Manager might prove useful in its entirety with respect to large-scale programs of this nature. Being able to have this sort of information so readily to hand can save a good deal of time in day-to-day program management. Furthermore, the intuitive ease of use and relatively small footprint of this software makes it suitable for running constantly alongside the other software applications used on a regular basis to support your organisational responsibilities. Let us return to the Document Manager and explore the final section which deals with invoices received.

The Invoices Received section works in exactly the same way as the other two sections, in that you may assign a document to the database with full details of its origin and the project to which it relates. You may make notes about each document and view it easily within the Document Manager interface if it is of a supported standard file format. Used in conjunction with the Report Manager, we may easily and quickly derive a sum total of all invoices received in association with a specific project (Fig. 6.8).

Having initiated a new record, we once again enter the specific reference for this document. This will typically be the supplier's invoice number. We must now choose the supplier from the appropriate drop-down list which will contain all the suppliers listed within the Supplier Manager database. In the Project field, we relate the invoice to a specific project by selecting it from the drop-down list box. In the Purchase Order Reference field, we may enter the purchase order to which this invoice pertains, thus creating a useful and fast process for checking the details of both documents. The date of the invoice, which may be the date the invoice was raised or the date it was received depending upon your preference, is entered in the Date field. The Total Value field reflects the total value of the invoice, and the File Location field functions as usual to identify precisely where this document is stored and allows you to quickly open it for viewing or editing within the Document Manager interface.

The Notes field enables the creation of free-form notes in relation to this particular invoice (using the text editor if you wish). Again, it is most useful, especially if discussions take place in relation to the invoice and you wish to log pertinent points accordingly. Once we have clicked on the Post Edit button, another document record is safely saved to the Document Manager database for subsequent evaluation within the context of our ongoing program of works.

The Document Manager, as we have seen, is extremely easy to use and yet offers quite powerful functionality. With a large program, we may generate literally hundreds of related documents, each one of which will be important in one sense or another. Being able to quickly identify and view any of these documents with just a few button clicks will prove extremely useful in day-to-day operations, especially when dealing with suppliers, application developers, business analysts, implementing agencies and the many others who might have an involvement with your program. Such functionality would be valuable enough in the context of running a small, self-contained project. When running a large-scale program containing many such projects, it will be especially appreciated. The document management software is often marketed as a separate, stand-alone application, and yet this functionality is included within the BANTAM Program Manager. In addition, the Document Manager complements the BANTAM application development methodology extremely well, enabling the user to quickly identify and reference any specific document.

6.3   Using the Report Manager

We now come to an equally valuable component of the BANTAM Program Manager software in the form of the Report Manager. As the name suggests, this allows you to create pertinent reports in relation to your projects (Fig. 6.9).

Perhaps the most unexpected feature of the Report Manager is its simplicity of operation. All of the hard work in retrieving data and formatting it into a coherent report is undertaken for you. All the user has to do is click on a button or, in some

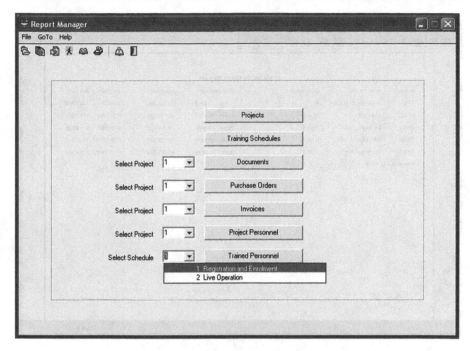

Fig. 6.9   The Report Manager main screen

cases, select a project or schedule and then click on a button. Don't let this apparent simplicity fool you though. The Report Manager is a very powerful and useful tool. With it, you can quickly produce reports around many aspects of your projects and view these on screen before printing them out on your regular printer. You may also save individual reports as a file for subsequent retrieval and analysis. All of this is via the simple and intuitive interface which is the Report Manager. Click on the Projects button and see for yourself how this works in practice (Fig. 6.10).

With a single click on the Projects button, the Report Manager has retrieved data about all the currently included projects and produced a summary report showing the project reference, project name, originating department, project manager, telephone contact number and start and end dates. It has also totalled the number of projects and date stamped the report for you. The report toolbar allows you to view the report in different ways, such as a whole page at a time, normal size or filling the available screen width. It also allows you to scroll through the report page by page, to go to the beginning or end of the report and of course to print the report directly to any connected printer. You may also save the report to file for subsequent retrieval, in either a special report format or, if you prefer, as a plain text file, enabling the report to be imported into a variety of other programs if so desired. This makes for a pretty versatile reporting system and yet, it remains extremely easy to use. A report of training schedules may also be produced with nothing more than a single button click. For the other reports, added flexibility is provided by enabling you to

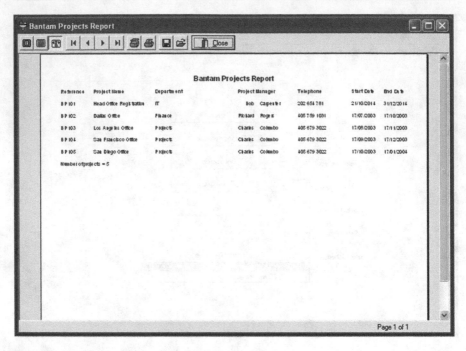

Fig. 6.10   The Bantam Projects Report shown on screen

filter the reports by projects or, in the case of trained personnel, by training schedule. This is equally intuitive and easily achieved via a simple drop-down list of
projects or training schedules from which to choose. Simply select a project from
the drop-down list to the left of the report button in which you are interested and
then click on the report button accordingly. The resulting report will be quickly
generated and displayed just as before, but the data included will only be relevant to
the project you have selected. Although the project is selected by project number, to
make things easier, the full project name is also visible in the drop-down list, ensuring that you cannot forget which project is which. If you have a large number of
projects active within the system, a scroll bar will appear within the drop-down list
enabling you to easily navigate to the desired project. Producing attractive, formatted reports really is as easy as that with the Report Manager tool. Let's try, as an
example, producing a report of documents associated with a specific project. First,
select a project in the drop-down list adjacent to the Documents button, and then
click on the Documents button itself in order to generate the report. You may be
surprised at just how fast this process is, considering that the data must be retrieved,
filtered and then formatted into a report ready for on-screen display and printing.
You will notice that the report is clearly laid out to show the document reference, the
document name, what type of document it is, who it was created by, the date of
creation and the precise file location where the document may be found. Having
such information neatly and readily to hand in association with specific projects can

prove invaluable when working on a large and complex program. A summary shows the number of documents and which project they relate to and, of course, the report is dated so we know exactly when this 'snapshot' was taken.

The other report types, for purchase orders, invoices, project personnel and trained personnel, work in exactly the same manner. Consider for a moment how useful it would be to be able to produce in an instant a list of all invoices associated with a given project, together with a total of all the amounts payable. The Report Manager enables exactly this similarly for purchase orders. This enables busy program managers to understand project costs without having to ask the accounts department every time. Equally useful is the ability to quickly produce a list of all personnel associated with a given project, including their department, physical location and contact telephone numbers. Once again, this information is available in an instant via the Report Manager.

Bringing a little order to a complex program is a desirable thing, a reality which even the ancient civilisations understood very well. The Bantam Program Manager software does just this, and the Report Manager module represents an important strand of this objective. It has been designed to be simple and intuitive in operation while offering succinct but powerful functionality. As a result, you will be able to use it frequently, tracking important aspects of your projects in a timely fashion without having to worry about the use of complex software tools. As we have seen in this section, using the Report Manager could not really be any easier. It is simply a point-and-click exercise, enabling a wealth of information about projects to be collated and presented ready for printing or saving as a file.

6.4 Using the Personnel Manager

The Personnel Manager is an important module within the broader program, as both internal and external personnel are necessarily involved in all aspects of running the projects which, together, constitute your operational portfolio. Other modules within the BANTAM Program Manager also access the Personnel Manager data directly, and so it is important to populate this database as early as possible, preferably as a first step, in your overall program life cycle (Fig. 6.11).

The operation of the Personnel Manager is extremely straightforward. Click on the Insert Record button within the lower toolbar in order to initiate a new personnel record. You may now fill in the relevant details and then click on the Post Edit button in order to save this entry as a new record within the database. The other buttons within the lower toolbar enable you to navigate throughout the database; to add, edit or delete records; to cancel and edit; and to refresh the data. A numeric indicator in the top right-hand corner of the screen shows a record number, which is useful for understanding where you are within the database. Another useful feature with regard to the personnel database is that if you select a project manager in the Project Manager module and then select the Personnel Manager module, the relevant project manager's details will already be selected within the personnel database, allowing you to understand who and where they are and how best to contact them (Fig. 6.12).

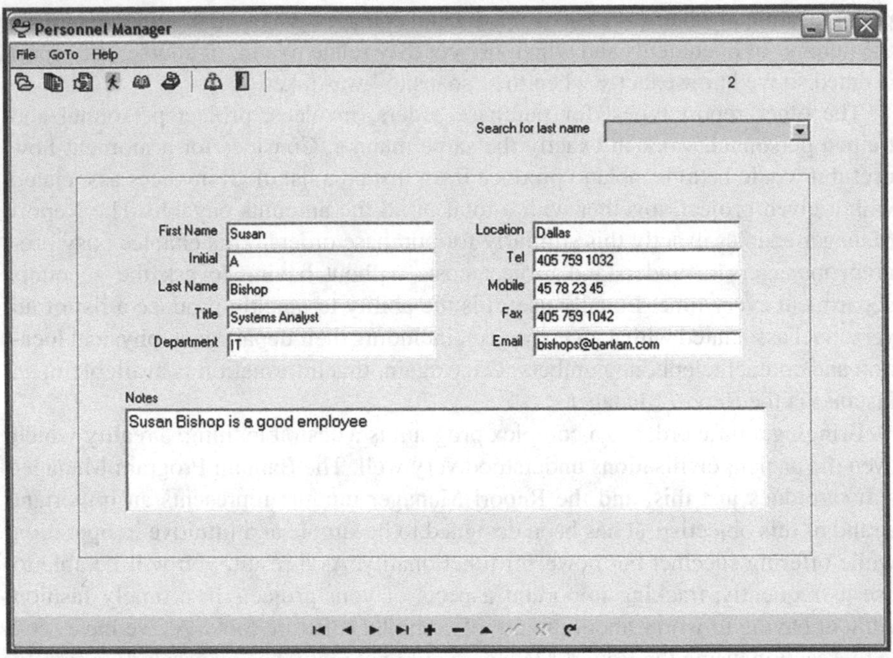

Fig. 6.11 The Personnel Manager

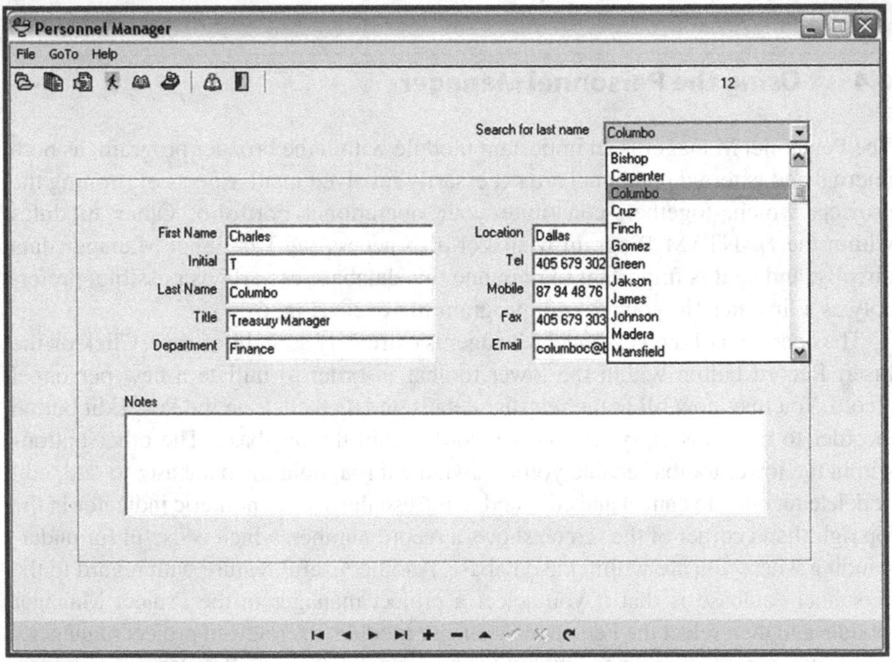

Fig. 6.12 Searching for an individual record

Another way of finding an individual quickly is to use the Search for Last Name drop-down box in the upper portion of the screen. Simply expand the list by clicking on the arrow to the right of the Name field and the last names of all individuals will be listed in alphabetical order. Clicking on the name in question will display the full details for this record within the main area of the screen. This is a very fast way of locating a particular record. The Notes section enables other information appertaining to the individual in question to be stored. By right-clicking in this field and selecting 'Edit', the text editor may be invoked which, among other things, will enable an existing document to be loaded into this field or the contents of the field saved as an external file. The navigation toolbar at the bottom of the screen provides the usual facilities for navigating among records, as well as adding, deleting or editing records as required. There is really not much else to say about the Personnel Manager module. It is extremely easy to use and, at the same time, extremely useful from a number of perspectives. Keeping all of your relevant contacts in a central convenient place is of course useful in itself. As a module within the BANTAM Program Manager however, the Personnel Manager is especially important as the other modules take information from the underlying database. For this reason, be sure to populate the Personnel Manager with care.

6.5   Using the Supplier Manager

Just as the Personnel Manager provides a useful database for all your in-house contacts, the Supplier Manager provides an equally useful central storage point for all of your external contacts. This database is also used by other modules within the main program and should be populated early within your program activities, although it is natural that this database will be added to over time as you discover appropriate technology or expertise and engage new suppliers accordingly. It is as easy to use and intuitive as the Personnel Manager, but does have some additional functionality which we should understand.

The principal difference is that the Supplier Manager is in itself a relational database with multiple tables, whereas the Personnel Manager is a single or flat-file database. The functional benefit of this is that you may enter as many contacts as you like in relation to one organisation. You may also categorise your main entries by as many organisational types as you wish.

You will notice from Fig. 6.13 that the Supplier Manager screen is effectively divided into three areas. The uppermost section provides the primary contact information for the organisation in question. The centre section provides a scrollable table of individual contacts, complete with their respective titles and department details. The lower section provides contact details for individuals selected within the centre section. You will notice also that there are two groups of navigation controls. At the bottom of the screen lies the navigation controls for the main organisational records. In the lower section of the screen, adjacent to the individual contact details, lie the navigational controls for the individual records appearing in the centre section. It is important to understand the relationship between these two

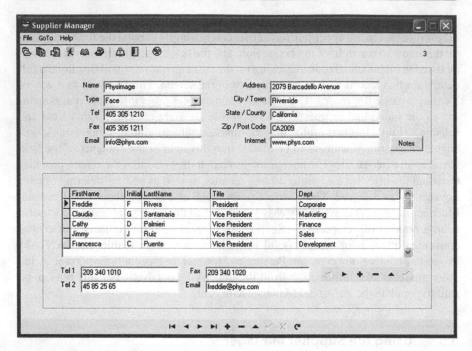

Fig. 6.13   The Supplier Manager main screen

sets of controls and how to use them properly. The main point to remember is that you must enter and save an organisational record in the uppermost section of the screen, *before* adding any individual records in the centre section. The reason for this is that individual records must be associated with a main organisational record; otherwise, they will become 'orphans' and you will not be able to find them again within the database.

To initiate a new organisational record, click on the Insert Record button within the navigation controls at the bottom of the screen and then enter the appropriate details within the fields in the top section of the screen. You will notice that the second field, named Type, features a drop-down list containing some typical types of organisation which you may wish to include in your database. Later on we shall see how to add to or edit these types. Select a type from the drop-down list and continue to enter data in the remaining fields. When you have completed all the fields for this record, click on the Post Edit button in order to save this record within the database. You may use the navigation controls at the bottom of the screen to select between main organisational records. With a main record selected, you may now enter the individual contact records for that particular organisation. Firstly, ensure that the main record has been saved. The Post Edit button at the bottom of the screen should be greyed out if the main record has been saved to the database. If this button is appearing black and active, then click on it now to save the main record before proceeding further. Now you may turn your attention to the second set of

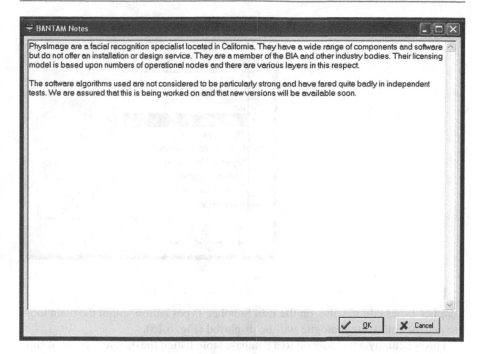

Fig. 6.14 The Notes field made visible from the Suppliers section

navigation controls within the lower section of the screen. Click on the Insert Record button and enter the name, title and department details for this individual. Enter the contact details for this individual in the lower telephone, mobile, fax and email fields, and then click on the Post Edit button in order to save this individual record. For the next individual contact record, click on the Insert Record button again and repeat the procedure. Please note that you must create a new record in this way for each individual whose details you wish to enter against the main record. As you add individuals, their names will appear as a list within the centre table.

We thus have all the information relative to a particular organisation neatly displayed within a single screen. The centre section will display up to six individual contacts at once. If you have more contacts for this particular organisation, you may scroll through the list using the scroll bar at the right-hand side of the table or, if you prefer, by using the navigation controls just below the table. Note that the individual contact details change as you select each individual within the table.

In the top section of the screen, there is also a 'Notes' button. This enables freeform notes to be entered and saved for this particular organisation. These notes are not visible on the same screen, as there is not enough space (this also enhances privacy), but may be checked at any time by clicking on the Notes button. Doing so will open another form, into which notes may be entered as appropriate (Fig. 6.14).

We mentioned earlier that the organisational type list may be edited in order to more accurately reflect your particular situation, and this is easily achieved via the

Fig. 6.15 Editing the
Supplier Types list

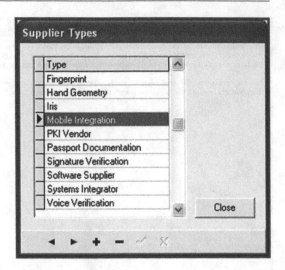

Supplier Types editor. Click on the Edit Supplier Types button within the main toolbar and the following dialogue will be displayed (Fig. 6.15).

This is actually a window on to a database table listing the different types of supplier. Using the navigation controls at the bottom of the window, you may add,
delete or edit a record accordingly. You may create as many different types as you
wish, but bear in mind that a smaller number of types will be easier to understand
than a larger number. If you edit a record, be sure to save your changes by clicking
on the Post Edit button. When you have finished editing this table, click on the separate Close button in order to return to the main Supplier Manager screen. Your
revised list of suppliers will now appear in the Type drop-down list, ready to be
selected as a field entry.

We have seen that the Supplier Manager is very easy to understand and use
and yet is also potentially powerful as a database in its own right. It is of course
also an integral part of the BANTAM Program Manager as supplier details are
drawn from this database to populate the drop-down lists within the Purchase
Orders and Invoices sections of the Document Manager module. Indeed, the
BANTAM Program Manager features the integration of several such modules in
order to provide a comprehensive view of your overall program situation. That
any one of these modules may be used as a valuable entity on its own may be
considered a bonus. The Supplier Manager certainly falls into this category as
you will find it extremely useful to be able to quickly navigate to a specific supplier record, see all the appropriate information displayed before you and be able
to quickly initiate contact if you wish. As the entire BANTAM Program Manager
consumes relatively little in the way of computer resources, you may wish to
leave it running continuously, providing you with supplier contacts at your fingertips throughout the day.

6.6   Using the Training Manager

We now come to an interesting and significant part of the BANTAM Program Manager. With regard to any application which features biometric identity verification checks, the importance of training cannot be overstated. Operational performance, in terms of error rates, is often directly proportional to the understanding of users and systems administrators, both at the enrolment stage and for subsequent usage. The wise program manager will ensure that training features prominently within the overall program plan. However, he or she will also wish to manage this aspect carefully, and this is where the Training Manager module comes in useful. The concept is very straightforward. Training is arranged into a series of training schedules, each one of which contains a number of modules which must be completed. Certification may be aligned with each training schedule and individuals may be assigned to a particular training schedule on a particular date. The Training Manager facilitates the creation and management of such schedules, together with a record of who has been assigned to what. Furthermore, the Report Manager may provide printed reports of who has been assigned to which schedule, together with their location and telephone number.

The BANTAM methodology is very well suited to the creation of training programs, as actual BANTAM maps for a specific application may be copied and used directly in relation to training for the same application, thus effectively reusing much of the expertise and work which went into designing the application in question. Indeed, one of the standard BANTAM documents is the Training Schedule document which, itself, references other existing BANTAM maps and documents. We can break this down to lower levels by the creation of individual modules within each training schedule, each with their own series of BANTAM documents as appropriate. All we need to do now is schedule the various training sessions and assign all relevant personnel to an appropriate session in order to ensure that everyone who needs to be trained is trained. The Training Manager makes this task easy with an intuitive process for establishing training sessions and modules, and subsequently assigning personnel to them on specific dates. Having all of this information readily to hand will prove invaluable to many organisations who have such a training requirement (Fig. 6.16).

There are two sections within the Training Manager, the Schedule Definition section and the Schedule Assignment section. They are selected via the two folder icons within the main toolbar. Hovering your mouse over these folders will activate a tool-tip label to show you which is which. In the Schedule Definition section, we may see the schedule reference and title, which operational process it is concerned with, whether any certification is associated with it and who created it and when. We may also see the details of the sub-modules which together make up the schedule and precisely which personnel have been assigned to it. This provides a succinct but very useful overview of all the training schedules you create for your program.

To create a new training schedule, simply click on the Insert Record button on the navigation toolbar at the bottom of the screen. Enter a schedule reference. This

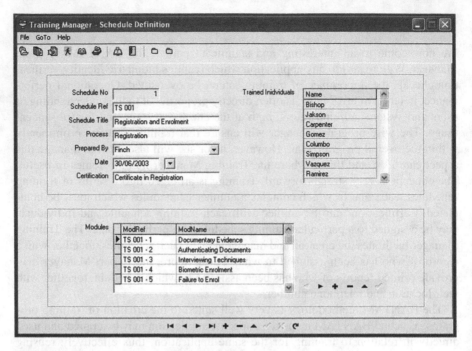

Fig. 6.16 The Training Manager main screen

will align to the Training Schedule document created for this schedule using the BANTAM methodology. Continue entering data into the Title, Process, Proposed By, Date and Certification fields and then click on the Post Edit button within the navigation controls at the bottom of the screen. You do not need to enter anything into the Schedule No. field as this is undertaken automatically. Similarly, you should not attempt to enter anything into the Trained Individuals list from this screen. Once you have completed the details for this training schedule and saved the record via the Post Edit button, you may now proceed to enter details of the modules which serve to make up this schedule. To initiate this task, click on the Insert Record button from within the smaller navigation set just under the Modules table. You may now enter the Module Reference and Module Name for each module, remembering of course to use the Post Edit button from within the smaller navigation toolset in order to save this information. Continue in this vein until you have entered all of your planned training schedules and their associated modules. You may now assign personnel to these training schedules.

Open the Schedule Assignment screen by clicking on the appropriate button within the main toolbar. The form shown in Fig. 6.17 will appear, ready for you to start assigning personnel to the various training schedules. This is simply achieved via the three drop-down lists within the top half of the screen. You do not have to type in any data and should not attempt to alter the table shown in the bottom half of the screen, as this is updated automatically when you create a new record. Click on the Insert Record button from within the navigation controls at the bottom of the screen. Now select in turn a training schedule, the member of staff you wish to

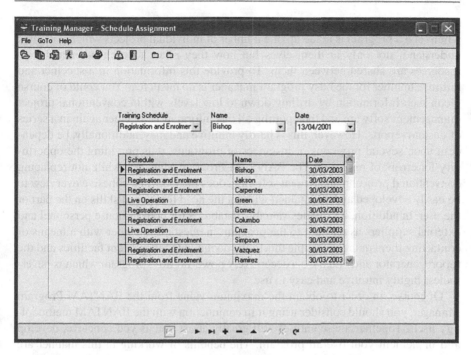

Fig. 6.17 The Schedule Assignment screen

assign and a date on which they will attend, or have attended, the schedule in question. Now click on the Post Edit button and this entry will be displayed in the table automatically. Go on to assign other personnel to training sessions in the same manner. The table in this screen will show all such entries for all training schedules. To see a list of which personnel have been assigned to a particular schedule, return to the Schedule Definitions section and use the main navigation controls to select a training schedule. The list of trained individuals will now be populated according to your personnel assignments. You thus have an easy way of keeping tabs on the various training sessions which have been created and who has been assigned to them. The training schedules themselves will be created using the BANTAM maps and related documents used in the actual definition and design of the application and its attendant processes. In such a manner, the BANTAM Program Manager integrates many related tasks and functions.

6.7 Conclusions

We have seen in the preceding sections how the BANTAM Program Manager is neatly integrated in order to provide you with the maximum information about your overall program, in the easiest fashion and with the minimum of effort on your part. However, the BANTAM Program Manager is more than just another piece of software. It is in fact a way of working which, once absorbed, will pay dividends with regard to the smooth running of your overall program. This is especially the case when such a program is made up of a number of individual projects which you must understand, not only in themselves but how they relate to each other and how resources are shared between them. To provide this information in a succinct and intuitive manner for the busy program manager is no mean feat. You could of course glean such information by drilling down to low levels within conventional project management software and then putting all this information together again in a series of custom reports. However, this is hardly intuitive and may, additionally, be dependent upon several programs or instances of programs, thus providing the opportunity for errors of omission. The BANTAM Program Manager, while not replacing conventional project management software, does provide for a cohesive overview to be easily developed and maintained without the need for special skills on the part of the user. In addition, it provides valuable databases for both in-house personnel and external suppliers as relevant to the program in question, together with a means of contacting them quickly. Couple this to the document management facilities and the report generator and you have a deceptively powerful little program which is nevertheless highly intuitive and easy to use.

Of course, in order to obtain the maximum value from the BANTAM Program Manager, you should consider using it in conjunction with the BANTAM methodology itself. Together, these entities will greatly assist you as you conceive, develop and implement your overall program. The benefits of working in this manner are many, some of which may be outlined as follows:

- The development of sound thinking around the special issues which are particular to applications which seek to introduce biometric identity verification checks within the larger application process.
- The strong documentation of all elements of both systems design and process development in a manner which may be shared among all parties concerned at any stage within the program, regardless of their individual perspective.
- The creation of systems design documents using an intuitive notation language which may be readily understood, regardless of spoken language barriers.
- The creation of a very comprehensive audit trail which clearly defines every element of the program, including roles, responsibilities and costs.
- The continual reuse of completed work for parallel purposes, leading to significant efficiencies in relation to the broader program.
- Considerable cost savings which come from a thorough understanding of operational issues, leading to realistic expectations. Coupled with sound application and process development, complemented by high quality training, these savings can be very significant.

This last point alone renders any investment in learning this approach particularly astute. If you configure the BANTAM Program Manager diligently and then use it on a day-to-day basis, you will find it an invaluable ally for the management of your overall program. Together with the BANTAM methodology and symbol notation, you will have a powerful set of tools at your disposal, with which to understand the nuances of all applications featuring biometric and related technologies. Importantly, you will be able to demonstrate all aspects of any project within the broader program, via a comprehensive reporting system, providing a valuable audit trail of events, design decisions, operational factors and costs. This will be particularly valuable for government agencies with large-scale public sector projects to manage and maintain. However, the BANTAM Program Manager may be used effectively, even in relation to small, stand-alone projects if required.

Additional Considerations

Within this book and in relation to large-scale applications featuring automated bio-metric identity verification checks, we have discussed technical factors, human factors and implementation factors. We have additionally introduced some utilities which provide valuable assistance to those involved in the implementation of such programs. However, before we get to the implementation stage, it may be useful to consider a logical progression from aspiration to implementation, highlighting some of the areas and issues of particular pertinence. We have touched upon some of these issues already, and, indeed, the regular use of the utilities mentioned earlier should encourage the reader to develop their own thinking in this respect. In this section therefore, we shall endeavour to place these factors in perspective, encour-aging the reader to develop a road map pertinent to their own particular situation.

Perhaps the first question to ask when considering an implementation of this kind is should we be doing this at all? Precisely why is such an initiative being proposed and are we sure that all other ways of achieving the objective have been properly considered? In this context, a detailed analysis of existing processes and their results would be highly appropriate. There is little point in developing a technological solu-tion to a perceived problem if we don't really understand the problem in the first place, or indeed, whether there is a problem at all. Sometimes, it is easy for depart-ments to get carried away with ideas around the possible use of technology, without striving to understand whether such a development really makes sense from the longer-term perspective. We have seen many examples of this where new develop-ments have been implemented, often in the interests of perceived cost reduction, and have subsequently had negative affects upon the organisation or department in ques-tion due to the impact upon both internal staff and external users or customers. The use of automated and/or shared call centres are one such example where much goodwill is often lost as a result of short-term greed. We see this in other areas of the organisation/client interface where attempts to force clients along a path, which is designed to be more convenient for the organisation, often result in that very inter-action and the associated trust being severely damaged. In many cases such a condi-tion could have been avoided with a little more thought and understanding of the realities of the situation. This point is stressed because the introduction of biometric identity verification checks into everyday processes, especially those in the public domain, and carries the potential for just such a misunderstanding if not properly thought through. We must be absolutely clear as to why such a development is being proposed in the first place, precisely what benefits are being anticipated as a result, to whom these benefits are thought to apply and what the potential operational impact might be. We must also understand whether any group of individuals might be disenfranchised in some way by such a development and, if so, what alternative processes are being considered for them. We should also ensure that, assuming there really is a problem to be solved in the first place, all potential solutions are properly considered, including manual processes which do not rely upon technology. If we do not strive to develop this understanding from the outset, we can be sure that the lack of such an understanding will come back to haunt us, often surprisingly quickly. The first step then is to be absolutely sure that the proposed development is necessary and has crystal-clear objectives, the implications of which have been properly considered from every perspective.

We may now turn our attention to the existing processes. Sometimes, understanding how these existing processes really work is no mean feat. Often they rely upon the experience and expertise of operational personnel who find ways around exceptions or clumsy procedures due to their acquired knowledge of the area in question. Such individuals often become adept at working with users, both in the corporate and public domains, understanding the issues that are most likely to arise and why. These are human-related factors which are not easily replaced by technology alone. Another item to consider is the overall impact that such developments might have upon the operation. For example, if the operational process is radically altered, this may result in operational job functions changing, possibly to the extent of creating redundancies and the need for retraining. If the proposed solution has not been adequately discussed with the affected personnel, this could create a rather negative atmosphere, not the ideal situation for introducing change. Similarly, if the user population are expected to change the way they interface with the organisation and this is not perceived as creating any advantage for them, then this may also create a negative response.

These are obvious examples of how people are affected by changing processes. There are often more subtle affects which it would be as well to understand. For example, suppose that Miss J who has now been relocated to another function or perhaps made redundant happened to be the only individual with a really good knowledge of how an associated process aligned with the one that has just been changed and was the person to whom others turned to for advice in this respect. The continuity has now been broken. This may be fine if the situation was understood and some contingency put in place but, if this wasn't the case, the introduction of the new process may not only have introduced new problems but may have also adversely affected other, dependent processes. We used a human-based example to illustrate the point, but there may be countless process- or systems-based opportunities for similar confusion. Suppose, for example, that a paper document that had been used in the original process had been subsequently used for other purposes as well, as it was convenient to do so. This is not at all unusual in the context of many organisations and processes. Now suppose that you do away with this document as part of your process re-engineering, there will be knock-on effects on the other process. One could think of many such potential occurrences and this is why it is so important to really understand the process you are seeking to replace, together with all of its interfaces and dependencies. When we introduce biometric identity verification checks into our broader process, are we replacing some other functionality? Are we altering the transactional flow? Are our operational personnel required to do something differently? The answer to this last question is almost certainly yes, depending upon where in the chain they sit. For many, there will be a whole new skill set to learn, especially for those involved in the registration process. They will need good-quality instruction accordingly. So will the ultimate users of the system, many of whom might be using such a technique for the first time.

You could paint a similar picture from the systems perspective. We must ensure that we fully understand the flow of data throughout the system, including any links to other sources and any associated dependencies, before we change anything. Such dependencies may not be immediately obvious to those responsible for your part of the operation. They may have inherited the current system without having prior knowledge of all of the associated links and interfaces. In such a situation it will be necessary to undertake a thorough analysis of the entire system in order to ensure that nothing is adversely affected by the proposed changes and that the optimum points are chosen for inserting the biometric identity check routines.

Having ascertained that we really understand both the existing operational processes and how they are supported by the in-place systems infrastructure, we can now turn our attention to designing the new processes. Often, this will best be undertaken by consultation with existing operational personnel, with reference to the proposed new process design. Fortunately, an ideal tool is available with which to accomplish this task, in the form of the BANTAM application modelling language. Simply map out your first draft of the new processes using the BANTAM notation language, and use these maps as discussion documents with which to refine the process until you arrive at the final process design, with which everyone concerned is comfortable. This final version may be documented accordingly as the reference from now on. Furthermore, in the spirit of component reuse, this same set of BANTAM maps may be used directly for training purposes. Indeed, the associated training requirements themselves represent part of the overall process design, as does the identification of human resource requirements for each element of the application. This should be equally detailed and fully documented accordingly.

Now that we have mapped out the processes, we might progress to designing the overall solution. Using BANTAM, we can map the high-level architecture as a starting point and then overlay onto this the biometric-related functionality. The beauty of using BANTAM in this respect is that we can systematically map lower levels of detail in order to show precisely how each functional requirement is implemented from a technical perspective, with each map interrelated to the whole. We can do this right down to code level, providing a well-articulated and documented overview of the entire application and its associated functionality. Once again, these maps will act as extremely useful discussion documents with which to check the understanding of current systems and how the current proposal will be best integrated. They will also provide the basis for subsequent technical training and associated maintenance manuals. Together with the process maps already created, we will now have a very detailed and extremely well-documented overview of both the current situation and our proposals for the new application. This may sound like a lot of effort, but it is an effort which will prove to be a very sound investment as we progress through the various stages of the project towards implementation. The evidence of this is reflected in our requirement specification, as we are now in a position to put together a detailed specification which reflects a well-considered and well-documented approach, with all perspectives taken into account. Potential technology suppliers will now be in no doubt as to the aspirations of the program in question and how we see the required functionality being provided. Furthermore, using the same BANTAM methodology, they may respond to individual maps and create their own proposals for delivering the application. The potential cost savings at this point are significant. The time saved alone, by going out to potential suppliers with a well-understood, well-considered and well-documented requirement, equates directly to cost. The reduced likelihood of misunderstanding, as we are all talking the same language, equally relates directly to cost. A high-quality requirement specification also makes it easier for suppliers and the client organisation to ascertain suitability for consideration. This specification should of course include clearly articulated objectives for functionality, operational performance and related costs, as well as clearly setting out the time frames for implementation. From here we can enter into preliminary discussions with potential suppliers.

An important step at this stage would be to initiate an internal communications program in order to explain the proposed application and solicit the views of those personnel directly affected by it. This can be a valuable exercise from several perspectives. Firstly, it represents a matter of courtesy to involve related personnel at an early stage of the project and make it clear that their views on the matter are valued. This will be appreciated and result in a more enthusiastic attitude towards the new proposals. It is worth remembering that many are cautious of change in their working practice or surroundings and we should be conscious of this reality. Secondly, it is sometimes surprising how useful such an exercise can be in generating ideas for enhancing the proposed application or otherwise streamlining its functionality and implementation. Often, the best understanding of a given operational situation is held by those who are on the spot. Gaining their confidence and support is important if we wish to introduce changes or enhancements to the current process. It also represents a valuable opportunity to check the understanding of the current processes and the skills associated with their execution. This can sometimes uncover some interesting factors of operation which may not have been immediately obvious from a distance. It is appreciated that designing and initiating such a communications program may be a non-trivial exercise in relation to large-scale public sector applications. However, it is an investment which is likely to pay future dividends in relation to the overall program.

As part of this internal communications program, we should also strive to understand if and how other departments may be affected by the proposals in question. In this respect we should ensure that all related areas are included in the communications activities and that there are opportunities to collect feedback accordingly. Once again, this can prove invaluable in uncovering dependencies and interfaces which may not have been obvious at the start. It can be equally valuable in understanding synergistic initiatives which may be planned by other departments, possibly offering opportunities for collaboration and economies of scale. The internal communications program is in fact a key element of our overall project. It provides many opportunities to establish the project on a firm foundation of understanding and support. As such, it should not be considered lightly but carefully crafted and orchestrated as part of our overall program.

Similarly, we should pay equal attention to our external communications program. This is especially the case for large-scale applications in the public domain. We must ensure that prospective users understand what is being proposed and why. We must also explain precisely how any changes in process will affect them personally and what they need to do, at what stage, in order to participate. We should ensure that they have every opportunity to ask pertinent questions or express their own views on the matter and, of course, treat such views seriously as valuable feedback, which indeed they are. In this context the Biometrics Charter Document and the Biometrics Constitution will prove invaluable. The former, in particular, provides the opportunity to communicate openly and honestly with potential users of the application, ensuring that all of their questions and concerns are properly addressed. Using this document as part of the external communications program will go a long way to promote goodwill and cooperation in relation to the application and its eventual introduction. In addition, undertaking this external communications program at the right time is very important. Users should not feel that they are being presented with a fait accompli, decided upon with little or no consultation, however important the objectives appear. A much better end result will be achieved if users are involved at an early stage, giving the implementing agency a chance to explain the objectives and why they are being pursued and, equally importantly, giving prospective users a chance to comment on the proposals and offer their own suggestions accordingly. Of course there will be some with extreme or distorted views influenced by their own agenda, but these will typically be a small minority. In the main, we can expect a reasonable reflection of the citizens' perspective in respect to our proposals. Indeed, this can be very valuable to the program overall as many good ideas often surface in such an environment of consultation and discussion.

At this point it would be useful to stand back and carefully consider all the feedback received as a result of both the internal and external communications programs. This should have been systematically collected and compiled, allowing for a list of concerns and suggestions to be produced and prioritised, based upon frequency and strength of comment. As previously suggested, it is quite likely that there will be some little gems of ideas buried here, just waiting to be discovered and refined into workable elements of the overall application. It is most important therefore not to consider such feedback as negative. On the contrary, this activity should be viewed as an integral part of your design program and supported accordingly. Each voiced objection, concern or suggestion should be carefully considered, ensuring that we understand exactly why such comments were made. Each element may then be considered with regard to potential impact and proportionality with regard to the overall program. This aspect warrants careful consideration. For example, a valid observation with regard to the operating environment may affect a high proportion of users and subsequent transactions. If such an observation is not understood, or worse ignored, this could have an unnecessarily negative impact upon the program. Similarly, with regard to human factors, expressed concerns and suggestions in this context should be listened to carefully and fully understood. It may be that some valuable alternative approaches might come from this. Do not assume that the systems designers and technicians have all the answers. In many respects, potential users and systems operators hold the most valuable information of all. It is vitally important that we solicit their views and act upon them accordingly. If we find that areas of serious concern emerge during this process of consultation, it is much better that we understand this situation now and have the opportunity to react to it, rather than find out the hard way after the application has been implemented. The accountant in you will also appreciate the cost implications of acquiring such an understanding after the event. If concerns do emerge and yet they do not seem clear, or perhaps otherwise ambiguous in their origin and expression, then it may be valuable to repeat the consultation process, if need be holding a special session to address a specific issue. This is the way to ensure that such points are properly understood and to reassure both potential operators and users that their views are taken seriously.

You may feel that we have laboured this point a little. After all, isn't it just a question of agreeing a technical specification and getting on with it? Well, the history of implementation of such systems shows us that this is not the case. Many systems have been introduced and then subsequently decommissioned as expectations were not met or the operation otherwise found to be unworkable in real terms. Many technology trials have been undertaken, only to be wound up and never to make the transition to implemented application. There are lessons to be learned here, many of them to do with human and environmental factors. Factors which will be unique to your particular application and its proposed scale. The technology suppliers and systems integrators may not have a robust understanding of these factors and certainly will not have the same perspective of those at the sharp end of operational processes. Consequently, it is vitally important to undertake these communications exercises and act upon their revelations. We should not be afraid to halt the design program at this stage and revisit it with new suggestions and ideas arising from our consultation with prospective users and operators. Indeed, if need be, we should be prepared to go back to the drawing board and start again. In any event, we should now carefully revise the application specifications, both from a technical and process perspective, ensuring that the resulting ideas from our communications and consultation exercise have been considered and, where appropriate, incorporated accordingly.

We have now tested our thinking with both the operator and user community and have a pretty good idea of how our proposals will be received in practice. We have also no doubt picked up many new tips and ideas from these discussions and revised our original high-level specification for both technology and process accordingly. Furthermore, assuming that we have documented all of this using the BANTAM maps and methodology, we are now in a very good position to approach selected technology suppliers in order to verify the feasibility of our technical proposals and refine the specification down to a lower level. This may be undertaken via a series of discussions and workshops which will include participation from our own technical support personnel. Discussions will be focused around the BANTAM maps, slowly developing each level of detail until we have developed a technical architecture which we are confident will support our intended processes and offer the flexibility and scalability we desire. To facilitate this contact with technology suppliers, we have standard BANTAM RFI (request-for-information) and RFP (request-for-proposal) documents, the use of which ensures consistency and encourages an equally consistent response. This is an important factor, especially when trying to understand suggestions and proposals from several different suppliers.

Hopefully, the reader has by now had time to take a close look at the BANTAM methodology and maybe even experiment a little with the various maps. If so, you will readily appreciate just how much time can be saved by adopting this approach. It is not just a question of time either. Consistency in discussion with different technology suppliers, a well-documented project archive and significant opportunities for reusability are all facilitated by the use of BANTAM. In addition, the provision of an interlocking series of maps with logical cross-referencing from a high-level overview down to the smallest technical detail, including application development, means that someone new to the program will be able to immediately understand how everything fits together and why it has been designed that way. This is true of both the technical architecture and the operational process. The value of this in real terms can be hugely significant. It also supports any internal quality assurance program which you may be running. From the technology suppliers' perspective, it will be extremely helpful to be able to discuss a well-documented proposal and to be able to respond, or make suggestions, using the same methodology. Furthermore, it supports their own archives and enables them to generate BANTAM maps for generic solutions, thus saving a good deal of time with respect to future projects while increasing their own perceived professionalism. Everything needed to use the BANTAM methodology is freely available from the Biometrics Research website. Readers are strongly encouraged to adopt this methodology. The small investment in time required to learn it will be repaid many times over, even in your first project.

Having gone through this process, we are now in a position to develop the final requirement specification, featuring a complete set of BANTAM maps and explanations, together with our tender documentation. Let's take a step back for a moment and consider the importance of this point. One of the biggest problems historically with programs of this nature has been a lack of clarity around requirements, leading to solutions which have sometimes not been a good fit. This in turn has often led to unwanted surprises in operation and, in some cases, the subsequent decommissioning of the application. In many cases, such a situation has been exacerbated by an equal lack of understanding of the associated human factors, leading to a level of realised performance far below expectations. Now compare this with the well-documented and qualified requirement specification which we have just been discussing. In our case, we have not only tested and refined our technical proposal to a point of high understanding but have echoed this with the proposed processes, in turn testing them with our operator and user communities, until we are confident that the overall proposal is workable and practical from an operational perspective. Together with an above-average level of documentation, we are now in a strong position to move forwards in a sensible and controlled manner. The next step of which will be to configure and issue our tender documents to the potential suppliers and technology partners in question. This tender should include a complete set of BANTAM maps, to which responding suppliers must confirm compliance or, if deviations are proposed, must produce complementary maps in order to show the proposed variances and associated consequences clearly. This ensures that we are all speaking the same language. Actually, when considering large-scale applications where responses may be received from foreign organisations, as is increasingly the case within our connected world, the use of BANTAM brings another powerful dimension in that the primary notation used is graphical and therefore spoken language independent. This guards against misinterpretation of both the requirement specification and subsequent proposals.

Once we have received all the responses to our tender and answered any associated questions accordingly, we shall now be in a position to choose a technology supplier or maybe more than one technology supplier, depending upon the application in question. It goes without saying that these suppliers must be able to demonstrate a thorough understanding of our proposed application, including both technology requirements and operational processes. They should also be able to understand the existing infrastructure and its attendant processes and how the new requirements will be absorbed into them. Their own detailed proposals should be documented using the same BANTAM methodology, with clear references to the BANTAM maps supplied with the tender documents. In this way, it is possible to compare like with like in a dispassionate and objective manner, without undue emphasis on presentation style or verbal explanations. If, from a perusal of their proposal, the precise technical and operational details are not crystal clear, one might well question such a response, as BANTAM facilitates just such a level of clarity.

When we have chosen our preferred suppliers and technology partners, we will now be in a position to draw up a final working specification, to which our application will be designed, built and implemented. Because we have used a strong methodology to orchestrate and document proceedings thus far, we already have in place a strong audit trail, showing exactly how our proposal was originally conceived, subsequently refined with consultation and finally developed into a specification for tender purposes. All of this information may be held within the BANTAM Program Manager application. Now we can complete the cycle with the preparation of this final specification, which should be a joint effort between ourselves and our technology suppliers. This preparation should include a double check of all related systems interfaces, messaging protocols and other technical dependencies. It should similarly include a confirmation and qualification of all operational processes. This final specification, duly documented using BANTAM, will also provide the basis for our technical and operational training material, providing a high-level or reusability while maintaining consistency throughout. There are obvious benefits here, not the least being associated with cost. With regard to training, as well as the subsequent maintenance and support of the application, this is also a good time to start developing the various training packages and planning for their implementation. In the context of a large public sector application, this can represent a significant task and should not be underestimated or under-resourced. This is not a matter of overkill; it makes very good sense to get this right at the outset and ensure that all training, for both operators and support personnel and users, is undertaken smoothly and in a timely manner to coincide with the introduction of the new application. Or, to look at it another way, getting it wrong can be hugely expensive and will impact negatively on the whole program.

When all this has been achieved, we are now ready to build and test the application in a test environment. When we are satisfied that, from the technical perspective, the application is robust, reliable and secure as well as meeting our required levels of operational performance, we can progress to the next stage. Precisely what this next stage is may depend upon the nature and scale of our application. For a large-scale application, we may well want to run a pilot installation somewhere in order to confirm the operation of the system and processes within a real live environment. If we decide to do this, we should clearly define our objectives for such a pilot and closely monitor all aspects accordingly. Transactions should be logged and analysed in a logical, repeatable manner. You may find detailed advice on running a pilot in the associated publication, *Biometrics: Advanced Identity Verification*, ISBN 1-85233-243-3, and later titles from the same author, also published by Springer.

One notable benefit of running a pilot system is to be able to experiment with settings within a controlled environment, noting their effect upon operational performance. This is especially relevant to the calibration of biometric capture devices. From this exercise can come a recommendation for device calibration which may be closely followed in subsequent installations. We shall probably also learn much about the physical operating environment from such a pilot, helping us to understand how this can affect transactional performance. We will of course already have a working understanding of the factors involved if we have used available utilities beforehand.

Assuming a successful pilot, we can now make any necessary last-minute revisions to our systems calibration or operational processes, ensuring that these are properly reflected in our training programs and associated material. We may now proceed to plan the roll-out of our application across all applicable operational areas and geographic sites. Depending upon scale, we may like to organise this as a phased approach, ensuring that each phase is successfully implemented before moving on to the next. We shouldn't have too many surprises in this respect as we have tested our proposal many times along the path towards implementation. Furthermore, everything is properly documented, facilitating a consistent approach to installation and configuration, reducing the probability of errors in this respect accordingly. One of the challenges in this context will be the coordination of the related activities such as training and the establishment of registration centres. Once again, because we have properly documented and configured these requirements, this process should be consistent and error free. However, we do have the human resource element to consider, and, with a large-scale program, this will require strong program management to ensure that everything is in place at the right time. The BANTAM Program Manager software should help you in this respect. In a multiple site system, consideration should be given to using the APEX centralised control software. This will ensure that all sites, and every node within a site, will be operating to the same standard and producing equivalent levels of realised performance, even if they are implemented and commissioned at different times and in different locations.

In conclusion, we have covered some of the salient points associated with the implementation of such a program. Naturally, each situation will be different and should be considered according to its own special requirements and objectives, but we have at least set the scene for a workable approach to such matters. The importance of proper planning and documentation cannot be overstressed. All too often we have seen large-scale applications in both the public and private sectors rushed into, poorly implemented and subsequently failing at a huge cost to all involved. The likelihood of this scenario, while worrying enough in relation to general IT projects, is accentuated when we introduce the additional complexities and human factors associated with biometrics. In addition, there is a public relations factor involved in such cases, again, accentuated by the inclusion of biometric identity checks. When things go wrong in relation to biometric systems, they *really* go wrong. It is paramount therefore that every effort be made to ensure that such a scenario doesn't occur. This book has provided an overview of the associated issues, together with an introduction to some extremely useful tools, in order to encourage a more considered approach to the implementation of applications which include biometric identity verification checks. It may be considered as a useful starting point for further deliberation. From here, using the tools and techniques thus far explained, the prospective program manager must strive to understand all aspects of the application under consideration, together with the anticipated impact of introducing biometrics into this scenario. Please note that, for wide-scale public applications, such an impact can be significant. If we are in the public sector, we have a responsibility to ensure that any such system is implemented in an ethical manner with full attention given to areas such as data protection and privacy. We also have a responsibility to be open and honest in our description of exactly how the application is configured and working, ensuring that there is no function creep after the event, with data being used for alternative purposes. Use of the Biometrics Charter Document will simplify matters considerably in this respect. In addition, we must pay particular attention to the security aspects of our application. This includes an understanding of the probability of fraud, attempts at identity theft, security of stored data, exception handling and revocation procedures. Thus, there are both technical and operational aspects to consider in this context.

The reader has by now understood that introducing biometrics and related technologies into everyday applications, especially those in the public domain, is an aspiration that should not be taken lightly. There are many issues to be considered, technical, environmental, process related and with regard to the associated human factors. There is a potential to get things badly wrong and to fail in the delivery of the anticipated enhanced security while simultaneously introducing new problems and potential security loopholes ripe for exploitation by those who may be so inclined. Having highlighted these and other issues, the reader is now in a good position to move forwards in a more considered manner, making full use of the tools and techniques outlined in this book. In the next section we shall discuss some of the application possibilities and related aspirations associated with the use of biometrics and related technologies.

7.1   A Brave New World?

We have been discussing the potential use of biometrics in everyday life for the past 20 years or so. Throughout that time, many ideas and concepts have been portrayed in a futuristic or high-tech light. This is curious when you think about it. After all, the concept of using a biometrics for individual identity purposes has been around for thousands of years. It is most certainly not a new idea. Neither is it particularly 'high tech'. The fundamentals of capturing an image of the biometrics and applying algorithms for encryption and matching purposes cover well-trodden ground. And yet, the public perception often remains one of futuristic technology imposed under a Big Brother or nanny-state regime, a perception encouraged by the movie industry who seem to delight in portraying biometrics in this way and government agencies who fall readily into the trap of maintaining secrecy around what they are actually doing and why. One feels sometimes that the biometric PR machine has not done too good a job in recent years.

It is interesting to consider how the thinking around applications for biometric technology has developed throughout this time. Initially, biometric devices were proposed as alternatives to tokens for physical access control applications, on the premise that you couldn't lose or forget your biometrics and, in any case, it was more secure than a token. With some techniques this worked well enough. For example, hand geometry lends itself quite well to physical access control in controlled environments. With other techniques, such as retinal scanning, for example, although the technology worked well, it was a little less intuitive in use and perhaps not as convenient as simply swiping a card. Nevertheless, the perceived higher security associated with retinal scanning ensured its use in various military establishments for access control purposes. Techniques such as voice verification and fingerprints were also employed in this manner, with varying degrees of success. Each of the primary biometric techniques could be shown, under controlled conditions, to work as a physical access control method, but some were clearly better suited than others, especially when deployed in real live environments. Perhaps it is not surprising therefore that the acceptance of these new techniques for physical access control was a little slow. Indeed, in the early years, hand geometry was really the only technique to achieve large numbers of deployed devices for physical access control purposes, with fingerprint devices coming a poor second, although both were also used for time and attendance recording.

In parallel, naturally it occurred to many that biometrics could be used to log on to computers. Early manifestations of this idea had two major flaws. One was the cost, with some devices costing almost as much the desktop computer they were supposed to be an accessory to. The other was the precise nature of the protection offered. If it was simply to inhibit the computer being booted, there were simpler and far less costly ways of achieving this which seemed secure enough for almost all purposes. If it was to interrupt the Windows operating system log-on process, then ways around this could be found which still gave access to system files. Many people therefore could not establish in their minds a cost and benefit value to using biometrics for computer access, even if they were fascinated by the technology itself. It took quite a while before a more carefully considered integration with the operating system was conceived and delivered, offering associated benefits such as data encryption. With the falling costs of fingerprint biometric devices, coupled to more refined matching algorithms, computer access started to look like an interesting application for the technology. Other techniques, such as keyboard dynamics, were also early entrants into the computer access scenario. But take-up was still slow. It has taken much longer to extrapolate this thinking into the design of a well-considered secure computing environment using biometrics as a personal identifier for defined access privileges for both local and network use. Indeed, we are still in the early stages of refining this concept, and take-up, while steadily increasing, is still nowhere near where some market analysts had predicted for this point in time. However, fingerprint readers integrated into mobile devices, particularly smartphones, are set to change all of that, due to the economies of scale in that marketplace and a different application model which will appeal to a different audience.

From the above we might usefully deduce that, while advances were being constantly made with regard to the biometric devices and matching algorithms themselves, the understanding of precisely how and why biometrics could be used in everyday working situations was somewhat slow to mature. Overambitious predictions of usage were constantly being made, leading to many start-up companies, some of which were unable to survive into the longer term as the expected business case simply didn't unfold in the manner expected. Other organisations understood that take-up would be slow and geared their operations accordingly, placing themselves in a better position for long-term survival, albeit with relatively slow growth. Another characteristic we saw at this time which reflected the position referred to above was a constant stream of operational trials. What this was telling us is that many organisations were fascinated by this technology but couldn't quite see how the application of it in their own environment might bring the benefits often claimed by the technology providers. Furthermore, they were not sure how the implementation of such technology would be accepted by the targeted users, whether they be employees or clients. This situation is still with us, perhaps in a lesser capacity, today. We are still seeing trials of biometric technology, some of which do not mature into working applications. This points mostly towards a lack of understanding around applications, rather than any fundamental faults with the technology itself.

After a while, we started to see ideas surfacing which focused more on the application itself rather than simply trying to find a use for the technology. This resulted in some more interesting applications in areas such as banking and even home shopping. We also started to see an increased interest from government agencies which leads to the technology appearing on drivers' licences and being used for benefit payments and other areas of public/government interface. Some of these applications were immediately successful and others perhaps more questionable, depending upon how well they had been considered. Furthermore, we started to see compulsory usage in some public application areas. This brings us to an interesting point around compulsory or voluntary use and the perceived levels of acceptance of the technology by users. This is an area which is sometimes the focus of much deliberation and concern by those seeking to implement such systems. It is also an area which is much misunderstood. It is not so much a matter of users being concerned or even against the use of biometrics per se rather a question of trust as to how and why such techniques are being introduced. Typically, if users understand exactly how a system is working and the reasons it is being proposed and that they additionally perceive the benefits of this proposal as worthwhile, then they rarely have any objection. On the other hand, if they have suspicions about how a system is working, how their personal data is being used and why such a system has been proposed in the first place, then they are quite likely to voice an objection. The concern is therefore usually focused much more on the application of the technology, rather than the use of the technology itself. This is an important point to consider as we develop our aspirations in this context. Of course, many applications, especially those in the public sector, such as border control, for example, dictate a compulsory use whereby individuals have no choice in the matter. Depending upon how such an application is communicated to users, this may cause a certain amount of resentment which, in turn, may impact the realised performance of the overall system.

So, where are we with applications of biometric technology today and what does the future look like in this respect? Let's start by looking at the current position. We have already mentioned the area of physical access control and this continues to be a solid application for biometric technology. We see this being implemented in government and military locations for high-security applications, on campuses for general access to facilities, at airports for access to airside facilities, in banks to separate public and private areas, in prisons for similar reasons, in corporate offices and many other areas. We also see variations on this theme. For example, a popular application has been for college canteens where students may be eligible for subsidised meals but need to positively identify themselves, similarly, for on-campus libraries. Another variation in prisons has been to identify prison visitors as they move through the facilities during visits. There are many other examples one could give, but suffice it to say that physical access control remains a strong application area for biometrics.

Access to computers and networks, sometimes referred to as logical access control, is another area of application which, while getting off to a slow start, has become an important focus for biometric vendors. Early implementations were perhaps somewhat crude and hard to justify on a cost basis, but the situation is now looking rather different with some very interesting possibilities. The reducing cost of biometric devices has played a part here, especially with regard to fingerprint readers, which may now be sourced below $50, making them more viable as an add-on computer peripheral. Integral fingerprint readers are featured on laptop computers for a while, although this has now become rare. In addition, the associated software and template matching algorithms have also improved, to the point that an average user may easily install such a device, enrol their biometrics and start using it on a daily basis with little trouble. Similarly, a busy network administrator within a large office may easily create a standard desktop configuration and roll this out quickly to a number of users with the minimum of fuss, although users will of course have to be enrolled and trained in the new logging-on techniques. This however is easily achieved with a little forethought and planning. Beyond this basic logging-on function, much thought is starting to be given to more sophisticated network security policies which may incorporate biometric checks at various points, with many quite comprehensive packages already available. These often integrate chip cards, USB tokens and digital certificates in a mix-and-match manner in order to provide flexible solutions for all manner of situations including access to Web services, intranets, extranets, remote network access and so on. Another continuing development which supports this concept is the integration of biometric readers into all manner of mobile devices. At present, these tend to be mostly fingerprint readers or facial recognition systems using an integral imaging device, but one can foresee interesting possibilities for other biometric techniques in this context.

We also have a number of functional specific applications. For example, there have been many trials of biometrics in relation to the use of bank ATM machines, some of which have been maintained in regular use. Different techniques have been tried and, interestingly, iris recognition has been a popular choice in this context, particularly with users. Biometrics have also been used very successfully in regard to social security benefit payments, where considerable savings have been realised due to claimants being deterred from multiple fraudulent claims or 'double dipping'. Indeed, it is a wonder that this application has not become more widespread, considering the potential benefits to the taxpayer as well as those legitimately claiming benefit. We have also seen the technique used for voting purposes, where we wish to ensure that an individual is not only who we believe them to be but that they only cast their vote once. Note that with these last two applications, biometrics are being used primarily to deter fraud, rather than for the provision of an operational benefit, although one could argue that there are also operational benefits involved. In a similar vein, we have seen biometrics appear on drivers' licences, in order to provide a mechanism to effectively bind the user to the document. This concept of being able to verify that the holder of a document is the person to whom it was originally issued is an important one which we shall see surface many times.

A particularly topical area at present is the use of biometrics in relation to national identity documents, a concept in which there is much interest from government agencies around the world. Indeed, many countries already have a national identity document based upon chip cards and biometrics. Views differ as to the benefits or otherwise of biometrics in national identity documents. In some countries, they are well established and consequently accepted as part of everyday life. In other countries they are viewed with suspicion and resentment. Perhaps this says something about the level of trust between governments and citizens in general. However, even in those countries who do not have a national identity document as such, citizens effectively carry identity documents in the shape of passports, drivers' licences and commercially issued documents such as bank and credit cards. Such documents are clearly aligned with the associated functionality. You require a drivers' licence in order to legally drive a car. You use bank cards in association with financial transactions, and you use passports in order to travel across borders. This brings us neatly to another topical application that of aviation security and border control.

The events of September 11, 2001, changed forever people's views about aviation and travel (however illogical some of the associated propaganda undoubtedly was). As enhanced security measures were considered and introduced, it was natural that the subject of biometrics would surface as a potential means of strong identity verification. One obvious area was that of physical access control between landside and airside or to specific facilities such as maintenance, stores and cargo. Biometric devices had already been used in this context and so it was a relatively straightforward matter to extend their use accordingly. Hand geometry was a popular choice of technique for this application in various locations, while fingerprints and other techniques were also used in specific instances. A potentially more interesting application in this context however was the use of biometrics in relation to border control. Immigration departments could foresee various benefits in being able to automate identity checks via the use of biometrics. On the one hand, such automated checks held the promise of being more consistent and reliable. On the other hand, the introduction of such ideas might relieve the pressure on human resources, freeing up immigration staff to concentrate on exceptions while regular, legitimate travellers enjoy an automated fast-track service. Furthermore, there would be opportunities to check these identities automatically against various databases and watch lists, alerting an immigration officer should something interesting be discovered as a result. In order to fully appreciate this thinking, one should understand the associated immigration-related controls such as the provision of API (advance passenger information) data, which is already a requirement for many countries, and the use of watch lists in order to screen passenger lists. From some perspectives, the use of automated identity checks using biometric techniques would seem to be a complementary extension of these existing controls. In reality, the situation is a little more complex than one might suppose, due to the nature of airline reservation systems and the multiple responsibilities involved in an end-to-end journey. However, the idea is firmly established and we have already seen a number of implementations, albeit with variations in scope, and we shall undoubtedly see more until travel anywhere will involve biometric identity checks. The primary reason that this particular application is so interesting is one of scale. While many implementations of biometric technology have been concerned with tens, hundreds and occasionally thousands of individuals, this application has a potential to involve tens or hundreds of millions of individuals. Nothing upon this scale, especially in terms of real-time operational transactions, has been attempted before and it will be particularly interesting to watch these developments as they unfold. Already, we are seeing some interesting tendencies emerge. Furthermore, there is an additional dimension in that a given individual may typically be registered in several such systems in different countries. This uncovers a raft of other issues around issuance, registration, scalability and interoperability which will be equally interesting to understand, as will the associated human factors. In addition, such an application sets a precedent for the wider use of biometric technology in relation to government services and the transactional interface with the citizen. Now we can appreciate why various governments are keen on the idea of a smart national identity card, incorporating one or more biometric templates. Passport agencies have been equally keen on incorporating biometrics. The next major application area may be that of payments using smart devices and a biometrics, although there are some caveats to such usage.

So now we are extrapolating our thinking from function-specific applications to a more general use of biometrics in a multi-application environment. We shall doubtlessly see the time when any important interaction with government services will require an identity verification check, using biometrics, in order to authenticate the individual as being eligible for the service in question. As many such services are effectively privatised, or subject to joint venture operation, this idea will bleed very quickly to the private sector and we shall see a similar requirement with regard to commercial transactions. Banking services and associated financial transactions are an obvious area, as are online transactions of various complexions. Automated debit and credit schemes using a token and biometrics will also surface. Indeed, this idea has already been trialled in a large supermarket environment whereby customers can effectively check out their own purchases without recourse to an assistant. One could imagine a similar approach in many environments, from filling stations to movie theatres and casinos.

A brave new world indeed, biometric verification checks are being undertaken in just about any transactional situation, with everything being automated in order to reduce manpower requirements and cut costs. The question is, is that really a good thing? Are we in danger of overemphasising the potential benefits of such developments? Are we equally in danger of destroying trust and encouraging a more sophisticated level of fraud and societal crime? These are questions which should be carefully considered by those wishing to implement wide-scale applications. We have already witnessed changes in attitudes, brought about by the use of such technologies in and 'us and them' scenario based upon mistrust rather than trust. This says much about our modern societies and how we have educated recent generations. As we take the concept further, what will be the further effect upon society? It is something that we should be thinking carefully about. There are those who would hold that the current level of 'Big Brother' control by the state (and commercial institutions) has already gone much too far.

Indeed, it is very tempting to think only theoretical benefits and application-specific functionality from the perspective of the implementing agency, without giving an equal consideration to the longer-term implications and consequences of such an implementation. We have already mentioned the importance of the registration process in this context and how, if this is not conducted to a high level of accuracy and consistency, the addition of a biometrics will not necessarily provide the anticipated enhanced security. It would be entirely possible, if wide-scale applications were handled badly, to simply move to a more sophisticated level of identity-related fraud which would prove much harder to detect and combat, with or without biometrics. We must therefore think very carefully about such developments and address some of the less obvious issues highlighted in this book and elsewhere. We must also consider the situation from the users' perspective. If biometric identity checks become commonplace in everyday transactions, and there is every indication that they will, the user may find themselves in a position of having to continually prove their identity when the automated process rejects them for one reason or another. Currently, the probable instances of such an occurrence vary from one technique to another but are in any event quite real. If operational processes are refined in order to reflect a high-confidence level in the biometric check, then it will be that much harder for a bona fide individual who has been incorrectly rejected by the system to prove their true identity. With wide-spread usage, this could be a frequent occurrence for individuals who, through no fault of their own, do not interface well with biometric devices. From their perspective, the introduction of such techniques will represent a backward step as they will see it as lessening their own quality of life. Depending upon the scale of this affect, we may find ourselves falling back on more traditional identity verification routines, thus negating one of the anticipated benefits of introducing this technology. Given time, the relative performance of biometric identity verification techniques will improve, alongside a corresponding wider familiarity of usage among citizens, leading to a more consistent user experience and, consequently, a higher level of accuracy in relation to individual transactions. However, this state of affairs may take some time to reach a critical mass and, in the meantime, we shall have to manage the developing situation most carefully. If we rush into wide-scale applications without fully understanding the broader picture, including human factors and user psychology, as well as the plethora of related technical and environmental issues, then we will be placing ourselves in a position of some vulnerability with regard to anticipated benefits and sustainability. In addition, we may be heralding in a new level of criminal sophistication before we are fully equipped to deal with it. This doesn't mean that we should not be looking to introduce such techniques where it makes good sense to do so but that we should think very carefully about the detail of their implementation and the impact that this will have, from a variety of perspectives. A well-considered implementation may be well received. An ill-considered implementation may do much harm.

Throughout the course of history, we have seen developments in technology, and the application of technology changes our society, our environment and even our cultural perception. Sometimes such change has been slower to manifest itself in reality than hindsight suggests. Often, those at the forefront of such change did not appreciate the eventual impact of the ideas they were developing and introducing. Such is the case with biometrics. The underlying technology is interesting enough, but it is the application of the technology and the associated process changes which will have a considerable impact upon society. It will change forever the way human beings relate to each other in a transactional context. It will change people's views about trust and human interaction. It will change individual's views about who they are and their place in society. It will change the relationship between state and citizen and between consumer and supplier. These are not small things.

Such thoughts may not currently be occurring to those technical boffins working on matching algorithms and biometric capture devices. They may not be occurring to those involved with marketing and selling the technology. They should be occurring to those, especially in government, seeking to introduce the technology on a wide scale. Given the eventual impact described above, we should be striving right now to ensure that any wide-scale applications in the public domain are carefully scrutinised from every perspective and that we are satisfied that related proposals may be implemented in an ethical, sustainable manner and with full consideration given to the associated human factors. Twenty or 30 years down the road, we shall see for ourselves the societal changes resulting from current ideas around the introduction of biometrics. We have in our hands a potentially powerful tool, a tool which, like most powerful tools, may be used for good or evil. We therefore have an attendant responsibility to ensure that it is used for the common good and to use our very best efforts to bring this about.

Throughout this book we have tried to draw attention to practical issues associated with the introduction of biometric technology to everyday processes. The freely available software utilities described earlier can be instrumental in developing the understanding of the reader in respect to this potentially complex area. This is not just another piece of IT to be subject to the same project management approach. The field of biometrics represents a peculiar mix of technology and societal interaction. The user of a biometric process is in fact a systems component, as they can affect realised performance just as any other systems component may, if it is not properly configured and understood. We may fine-tune the systems components under our immediate control as part of the application development and final commissioning process. We do not have quite the same level of control over the human component. We cannot therefore predict so accurately the real-world performance of a given application, due to the variability of this critical systems component. The best we can do is to try to understand this component and the variables and methods that it encapsulates. We may then consider how these variables are activated and what effect they might have upon transactional performance. This is why we must understand user psychology and all the associated human factors. Beyond this, we may care to extrapolate our thinking to the broader picture and the societal change which the introduction of widespread biometric identity checks will undoubtedly produce. A brave new world? A new world certainly. Its precise complexion however lies in our hands. Let us bring our best endeavours of craftsmanship and compassion to the task.

7.2   Keeping Things Simple

A good rule of thumb as we move forwards is to strive to keep things simple. This includes not just our technical designs and associated operational processes but our aspirations in general. It sounds obvious, doesn't it? And yet one might be surprised how often a relatively simple concept such as the introduction of a biometric identity check can become complex out of all proportion to the perceived issue. We start off thinking about the biometric technique to be deployed and are in no time thinking about shared databases, replicated servers, digital certificates, establishment of third-party certificate authorities, wireless communications and all manner of things. Before long, we have conceived a 'solution' which will probably cost more to implement than the original application and will involve additional human resources and associated ongoing costs. Indeed, those who let their enthusiasm run away with them in this respect have usually long since forgotten the original requirement by the time they reach this stage. Another complication which needs to be kept in perspective is that of security. When we start considering all the ways in which such a system could be circumnavigated, such as dummy body parts, replay attacks whereby we inject the 'valid result' tag into the system, even an incorrect biometric template in order to match against an impostor, etc. Of course, all such things are possible, but we have to match the practical probability of such an occurrence against the risk involved. In some cases of very high-security applications, perhaps in military environments, for example, we may well wish to look at these issues in some detail, but for many applications, we will be faced with the reality that no system is going to be perfect and that, in any case, the determined fraudster will take the path of least resistance which, for many applications, is unlikely to be turning up at your biometric reader point of presence with a collection of dummy fingers and irises and a truckload of computers and test equipment, especially if such a point of presence is manned. There are usually much easier ways of committing a fraudulent identity transaction, including simply registering your biometrics against incorrect demographic data in the first place, something which is all too easy to achieve in many countries. I am not suggesting for a moment that we do not consider such issues at all but that we merely place them in context of the application at hand.

To look at this another way, consider an application which is already working well, with well-considered operational processes, which everybody concerned understands, to which we simply wish to add a biometric identity verification check. There is little point in turning the application on its head, rewriting all the processes and introducing several additional layers of technical complexity, if it is not going to achieve a significant functional benefit. It is all too easy to fall into the trap of adding technology simply because it can be done. A better approach would be to consider the minimum amount of technology and change which could provide the sought-after additional functionality. The starting point for this is a robust under-standing of the existing process and why we think that the addition of a biometric check would improve the situation. This needs to be a qualified conclusion based upon current transactional evidence. For example, if, within a given process, we are experiencing a high level of identity fraud, then this can be quantified, together with the projected cost of this situation. Similarly, if we are anticipating an unmanned automated check to replace a manual process, perhaps on the grounds of transac-tional speed or human resource efficiencies, then this should be quantified accord-ingly. Now we can align the projected costs of implementation against the benefits expected and make a business case for our proposal. If the business case makes sense, we can then concern ourselves with the practicalities of introducing such a check, including the most appropriate technology and the optimum place in the overall process for its introduction. From here, we can consider the technical aspects of systems integration and practical operation, always looking to achieve the mean in terms of technical complexity. Mapping the existing processes and application via the BANTAM methodology will prove invaluable in this respect, as it will help to visualise exactly where and how the biometric functionality might best be incorporated.

Let's start with the biometric capture device. Having chosen our preferred bio-metric technique, we are now in a position to evaluate capture devices and choose one which is appropriate to our environment. In the vein of keeping things simple, what we should be looking for here is consistent, reliable operation and an easy interface to our host system, using established standards wherever possible. Beyond this, we need few bells and whistles in a capture device. We shall of course have to physically integrate this capture device into our operational environment, which may be a kiosk of some kind, a working desk, an entry point or some other point of presence. Here is another area where elegant simplicity will pay dividends, the user interface. Consider a kiosk, for example. If we are communicating with the user via a touch-screen display, we have an opportunity to create a visually attractive but highly intuitive interface with clear, plain language prompts which leave the user in no doubt as to where they are in the process and what they need to do next. We don't need flashing lights or sophisticated animated graphics, just simple, plain prompts presented in an attractive manner, which everyone can immediately understand, an obvious requirement perhaps and yet one which is often not fully met.

We can pursue this thread into our systems interfaces and related processes. If what we want is a biometric identity check at a certain point within a transactional process, then let us consider the simplest way of achieving this. In many cases, this will be facilitated by a branch in the software flow, accompanied by prompts and waiting for a returned result before continuing the original process. Of course, we shall need exception handling routines which, in many cases, will simply mean reverting to a manual process and prompting the user or operator accordingly. A key question is precisely where the biometric matching process takes place and from where the reference template is acquired for this purpose. In a simple scenario, the biometric reference template may be either resident on a portable token such as a chip card, for example, or perhaps in an internal database within the biometric capture device. Either of these options provides for a relatively quick matching process without reliance on external systems components. The alternative is for the reference template to be stored within a central database and called up for matching purposes against the live sample. This may be undertaken at the database position or at the biometric reader position. In either event it will require a biometrics to be transported across the network. If we use a central database, we shall probably wish this to be replicated somewhere in the interests of security and continuity. In a large application, such a database may be replicated or distributed among several distinct locations. As we can see, there are layers of potential sophistication or complication, with respect to this one factor. When we extrapolate this across every factor, we shall equally discover potential variations and options, hence the desirability of striving to keep things simple, wherever possible. Every layer of complication brings with it operational variables and associated opportunities for errors. The same is true of attendant processes. If we keep these straightforward and intuitive, we shall be rewarded with consistency of operation. If these are unnecessarily complex, we shall introduce additional opportunities for errors. It is perhaps not necessary to go through every example and instance where this may apply but simply to draw attention to the concept and let the reader apply it in their thinking as appropriate.

Having worked through this book, the reader is in a good position to strive for simplicity as he or she can use the concepts and methods described in order to fully understand the processes, issues and technicalities involved. With respect to wide-scale applications, some time spent on understanding scalability will additionally serve to highlight the importance of striving towards elegant simplicity in both design and implementation.

One might initially find it strange that such a subject is dwelt upon within this book. However, I have no doubt that many who have implemented either technology trials or actual applications featuring biometric identity checks will, with hindsight, fully endorse this philosophy. There are enough variables associated with the fundamental concept of using a biometrics, without adding to them with layers of complication where it is not absolutely necessary. The 'keep-it-simple' philosophy is a valuable one in any operational technology context. In the case of integrated biometrics, it is especially valuable.

7.3 The User Perspective

We have spoken at length at about the issues affecting the implementation of applications which incorporate biometric identity checks. We have additionally stressed the importance of working closely with prospective users and the importance of understanding user psychology and how it can affect operational performance. Perhaps it is pertinent also to consider the user perspective in broader terms. How do people really feel about using biometrics? We know that in some circles there is a concern, often expressed in relation to the use of biometric templates and how they might be used. Some of these concerns are simply around the fact that people do not like the idea of governments or third parties holding images of their faces or finger-prints in databases, especially when the reasons for doing so are not always clearly articulated (vendors used to argue that they shouldn't worry as images of the actual biometrics were not stored but algorithmically derived data representations which could not be reverse engineered in order to produce the source image. However, this argument is looking increasingly weak as the majority of current and proposed applications, including those on a wide scale, are indeed seeking to store the bio-metric image). Other concerns are focused on identity theft and whether the inclu-sion of a biometrics may make it harder for a victim to prove their true identity. In this respect, there are arguments both for and against the use of biometrics, but few of them have a strong scientific foundation. There are also more fundamental con-cerns around what many see as an increasing 'Big Brother' syndrome with the state making more and more impositions upon citizens and having too great an influence upon their private lives. Indeed, privacy seems to be a disappearing concept, although many would claim that it is a fundamental human right.

Against such concerns, those seeking to introduce biometrics into the civil equa-tion claim that citizens no longer have any such rights to privacy and that, in the fight against terrorism or more general crime, all such measures are valid. Many respond to such arguments with statistics which show that, even with all these 'Big Brother' technological developments, such as closed-circuit television, access con-trol, biometrics and more, crime is at an all-time high and showing no signs of receding. They would claim that the way to tackle rising crime is to address the societal situations which give rise to it in the first place, many of which are ironi-cally orchestrated by the same governments who seek to introduce advanced tech-nological measures to fight crime. These somewhat chaotic discussions, claims and counter claims show us that the use of advanced personal identity verification tech-nology for public applications is a concept capable of arousing emotive responses. Perhaps the pertinent issue at present is how clearly and honestly such responses are addressed, together with the qualification of related claims and explanations. This is precisely why the Biometrics Constitution and Biometrics Charter Documents have been developed. They are freely available from the Biometrics Research website.

Human beings are complex entities. We walk on this earth but for a short time, absorbing the culture, attitudes and events which surround us for this brief window in history. Our particular understanding and point of view is influenced by many things, from early childhood onwards. Add to this melting pot, individual character and natural inclination, shaped by opportunity and, some would say, fate and an individual perspective on life, start to develop. Multiply this by hundreds of millions of individuals and things get even more interesting. Some of these individuals lead charmed lives and never experience intense emotions. Some of them fall on their feet and are relatively successful in the game of life, without really knowing why. Some of them are ruthless and inherently dishonest in their dealings with life. Some of them are victims of circumstance or other people's ambitions. Some lead lives punctuated by tragedy and sadness. Some are familiar with the depths of loneliness and depression. Some are cheated by ill health or physical deformities. Some are sent to entertain us. Some repel us. Some are magical. Within this incredibly diverse tapestry of human kind, it is a wonder that we find consensus on many things. But we often do. It is as if there is an inherent common understanding which will, sooner or later, find expression no matter how much some may try to manipulate it. Therefore, when people raise concerns around fundamental concepts, even if these concerns are fairly rough and ill defined, it is as well to listen to them carefully. Such is the case with the wider-scale use of biometrics. While many will simply accept such developments as an inevitable sign of progress, we cannot ignore the fact that many more are equally voicing grave concerns over the wider-scale deployment of such technologies. We have a duty to listen to and understand these concerns and take them into consideration when developing ideas for introducing biometric identity checks into everyday processes. In many cases, such concerns may be borne out of ignorance of how the technology works or precisely what operational processes are being introduced and why. This gives us an opportunity to address such concerns honestly and openly, explaining our rationale for seeking to introduce the technology and inviting informed discussion around the associated issues. This would be a sensible way forwards and, as already suggested elsewhere in this book, may actually provide us with some valuable suggestions for refining our operational aspirations. On the other hand, those who choose to ignore user concerns and push ahead with their plans with little or no consultation may simply be setting themselves up for some spectacular failings further along the line.

The user perspective also surfaces in relation to the more physical implementation of such ideas, specifically with the physical user interface and the perceived operational processes. Creating an intuitive and attractive user interface may not be especially difficult, and yet it is an area that many get badly wrong. It is not just a question of operational software, such as might be used in a kiosk, for example, but the entire operational environment and user experience. This may include external factors such as lighting and temperature, as well as mundane items such as signage and visibility of the point of presence. In addition, we have the physical operating conditions relating to the biometric capture device to consider. None of these factors are particularly difficult to understand or to respond to in our application design. But they do require a certain attention to detail, especially if the overall effect is to be a positive one. In this respect, we need not only to understand the user perspective but to anticipate it and cater for it accordingly.

We thus have two broad areas to consider. On the one hand, we should ensure that we understand the views of our prospective users and take the trouble to explain to them the rationale behind our aspirations and exactly how the proposed application would be implemented in practice, addressing along the way all of the emotive issues around individual privacy. On the other hand, we must equally consider the user perspective in relation to operational reality. In this respect, the performance and repeatability of individual transactions may be severely compromised if we do not pay sufficient attention to this area. Neither of these areas is difficult to manage, providing that we are sincere in our aspirations and open about our plans to implement them. We have a societal responsibility in this respect which we must take seriously. Applications currently deployed and others under consideration have the potential to affect the lives of millions. Citizens will become more aware of these developments and many questions will be raised in both social gatherings and public debate. We must ensure that such developments are intelligently conceived and that their deployment is undertaken in an ethical manner, sensitive to the views of the majority of law-abiding citizens. The key to this is open and honest communication coupled to a robust understanding of the user perspective. Every proposed application should have an associated Biometrics Charter Document which should be shared openly with all prospective users and others interested in the application at hand. This document, in turn, should be informed by the Biometrics Constitution.

7.4   Conclusions

The title of this book is *Practical Biometrics*, and we have consequently focused a great deal on what it takes to design and implement an application which features biometric identity verification as part of its operational process. However, we have also covered many of the less obvious issues and tried to draw attention to some of the human factors peculiar to this sector. The science and technology of biometrics is one which is inexorably bound to the user, both in concept and actual operation. We must therefore be more than simply systems designers in order to conceive and implement a successful introduction of biometrics into an existing or new process. We must equally be psychologists and perhaps even social philosophers if we are to excel in this task. Within this book, we have drawn attention to this in many ways and provided tools and information to assist with the development of a robust understanding in this context. The reader may now take this as a starting point along the road towards their own special understanding as befits their particular sphere of operation.

A casual observer may be inclined to underestimate the importance of this whole area. However, as we have previously stated, the introduction of biometric identity verification techniques will have far-ranging consequences. Until relatively recently, such developments were mainly restricted to closed-loop systems in military, corporate and some academic scenarios. We now live with the reality of much larger public scale implementations which affect the lives of millions. Along the way, there will be some abject failures, some notable successes and some implementations which will achieve little and cost much. They will all come to public attention and the media will publish reports both for and against the principles involved, mostly based upon emotive sensationalism rather than any scientific grounding. Among all of this, the fact remains that we are entering a new era of personal identity verification in relation to public and commercial transactions of all kinds. This is not just a matter of technological development but a fundamental rethink in societal trust and how we interact with each other. In this respect it may not be an understatement to say that things will have changed forever. As a reader of this book, you may well have a part to play in this state of change and therefore an attendant responsibility, as we all have, to try to ensure that such developments are not rushed into blindly, or under the pretext of adherence to another agenda, but are properly considered and implemented in an ethical and responsible manner. The concept of biometrics has been a long time coming. It is now well and truly with us and we must deal with it accordingly. One can see many positive attributes to the use of this technology. One can also see the potential for much misunderstanding and over-stated expectations. When implementing applications in the public domain, once introduced, specific operational techniques and processes will be especially hard to change. We must therefore strive to ensure that any such applications are designed with our very best efforts and with due respect to in-place standards. This affects the biometric technique chosen, the manner in which the biometric template is pro-duced and stored, the token (where applicable) used to carry the biometric, the mes-saging format used in communications, how and why data is shared and much more. In addition, we must also appreciate the strengths and weaknesses of supporting IT infrastructures and how this affects our aspirations as well as actual deployment.

A few years ago, those interested in science fiction and spy movies used to love to refer to biometrics and feature such concepts in their stories and screenplays. Now they will have to find something else to focus upon. Biometrics are no longer science fiction. They are science fact. The next chapter will focus upon technology futures and the implications thereof, leading logically from the practical deploy-ment issues so far discussed.

Technology Futures

8

In our modern world, technology is constantly evolving, driven by business models which are founded fundamentally upon the concept of constant change. Consequently, whatever the application, the underlying technology will be subject to change. This does not necessarily mean that all such changes should be adopted; indeed, the intelligent implementing agency will not rush to embrace technological change for its own sake. Nevertheless, there is a tendency, among both government and private sector enterprise, to be swept along by the tide, without stopping to question the logic (or cost) of technological change. There is a parallel tendency, among technology providers, to introduce new technology simply because it is possible to do so. Having found a new technological paradigm, it is not difficult to weave a marketing campaign around it which will convince the gullible that they must adopt the new approach. We have seen this again and again in the world of information technology, and the trend shows no sign of abating, even though, in real terms, many organisations and government agencies are effectively going backwards in terms of efficiency of operation while incurring ever-increasing costs. There are various sociological reasons for this, which lay beyond the scope of discussion within this chapter. Instead, a focus will be brought to the implications of such a technological model and what this means from the perspective of identity management and, in particular, biometric identity verification. In this context, we are on the cusp of some significant changes which will render the use of biometrics more pervasive. From payments to automobile access and from national identity to identity verification in relation to almost all personal transactions, we are going to see biometrics used everywhere and the efficacy of operation across applications will be hugely variable. In addition, a new wave of fraud will emerge, based upon the notion that a biometric identity verification transaction may be trusted, which will prove quite difficult to pin down and eradicate. In the background, technology suppliers and implementing agencies will be crowing about security and biometrics and why their use is absolutely essential, even for everyday mundane transactions. The reader may draw their own conclusions as to whether such developments are really in the interests of the common good. In any event, this is the way things are

© Springer-Verlag London 2015
J. Ashbourn, *Practical Biometrics*, DOI 10.1007/978-1-4471-6717-4_8

shaping and we need to understand the implications. We also need to keep one step ahead, technically speaking, in order to ensure that we do not inadvertently introduce security weaknesses that were not previously present and which will tie up precious resources in their resolution. Similarly, some of the newer developments have significant implications for users, both from an enrolment perspective and for general usability in terms of the user interface and the interaction with other applications and services. This, in turn, creates a more confusing picture for the purposes of ongoing management.

8.1   The Mobile Explosion

Perhaps the most significant development for users in recent years is the explosion of mobile devices, from phones to smartphones to tablets and a variety of hybrid devices with touch screens and various appendages. The parallel development of a multitude of downloadable 'apps' ensures that there is always something new that users can try with their mobile devices. In addition, the devices themselves have in-built obsolescence, with new models appearing, one after another in a solid stream of high-pressure marketing to ensure a steady churn of devices and, of course, costs. As part of this continued development, biometrics have come into the picture, both as applications for mobile devices that use the inherent transducers already present on the device and as dedicated functionality embedded into the core of the mobile device itself. In the former category, there are a variety of facial recognition, voice verification and other applications, of varying efficacy. In the latter category, dedicated fingerprint recognition technology is becoming widespread. This may be implemented via discreet fingerprint readers on the device or via the integral touch screen and appropriate software. For facial recognition and iris recognition, the integral camera devices inherent within the majority of mobile devices may be employed, together with appropriate software. However, the resolution and dynamic range of the imaging transducers found on these devices can be somewhat variable, both across products and even across samples of the same product. This makes it difficult to achieve consistent levels of performance if user-owned devices are used within a broader application. A similar situation exists with respect to the microphones used and their optimisation in terms of bandwidth and dynamic range, which may or may not suit voice verification programs particularly well. Furthermore, with both image and audio transducers, their operation may be affected by the physical environment in which they are used. Incident and reflected light will affect imaging devices, and background noise and reflective or adsorptive surfaces will affect audio transducers. In both cases there exist a number of environmental variables which may affect the efficacy of a biometric identity verification transaction.

In addition to the environmental factors appertaining to the use of mobile devices, there are of course a whole raft of user factors which will introduce considerable variations in the interface between the user and device from a transactional perspective. All of the issues previously described under user factors and user psychology will apply but will be further accentuated by the very nature of mobile devices and the unpredictability around where and how they will be used. Depending upon the matching algorithms used, it may be difficult to achieve a high level of accuracy with respect to the matching of the live biometrics and the stored reference, due to this inherent variability of use. With conventional matching methodologies, it is likely that relatively low matching thresholds will be employed in the interests of remaining user friendly. This means that the probability of false positives may be rather higher than we would like. If the Proximity Matching Method is employed, this will be less of an issue. Another, fairly significant issue with mobile devices lies around the registration of the reference biometric sample. In the vast majority of cases, this will be left to the user themselves, introducing another level of variability. Some users will have a reasonable technical understanding of the process and may be fairly disciplined in the way that they undertake the registration function. Others will simply blindly follow the device manufacturers' instructions, possibly, while in a quite unsuitable environment. And others may not even follow the instructions properly. The result will be a wide variation in the quality of enrolled reference templates that reside on mobile devices. If fixed matching thresholds are employed, this will result in transactional errors which may have been avoided within more closely controlled applications. Such realities should be taken into consideration by those deploying applications which will allow biometric identity verification via user-owned mobile devices.

There is an additional security risk inherent in the mobile model, in that the user effectively controls the claimed identity as well as the biometric functionality. A mobile device may be registered to an individual but used by another. The operator of an associated application will have no knowledge of this, assuming that the registered user is the actual user (assuming of course that even the registered data is correct—a big assumption). Currently, most devices fall back to a simple password, should the biometric capability fail. Thus, a non-registered user who acquires this password might usefully re-enrol his or her own biometrics and then use the device in a transactional sense, effectively pretending to be the registered user and consequently defrauding the application. The notion that the addition of a biometrics proves the correct identity of the user is rather ambitious in this context. It may well be that a majority of users use the functionality properly and may be relied upon to do so. However, those with more malicious ambitions may find a whole new world of possibilities open to them via the widespread use of mobile devices. We need to be cognisant of this reality and consider the end-to-end security of transactions conducted via mobile devices in some considerable depth. There will undoubtedly be a rush to incorporate biometric technology into every mobile device and thus promote such devices for use in interactive transactions, including those involving payments or the transfer of funds. In addition, there will be a drive to use mobile devices as personal identity verification devices in their own right, for a number of purposes. This may be fine, providing that we properly understand the level of risk involved. The risk assessment should include the possibility of loss and theft of the device in question and the probability that an attempt will be made to use the device maliciously. In short, biometric identity verification on a mobile device is an entirely different proposition from that upon a fixed infrastructure and carefully controlled administrative process. It would be unrealistic to harbour the same expectations of both environments. This doesn't mean that we should not entertain the use of biometrics on mobile devices, but simply that we should properly understand the implications of doing so. As with any application, we should carefully consider and design the attendant processes, the technical architecture and the end-to-end data flows and operation. We should also develop some precise guidance for users, including how to register a good-quality biometric reference and how to understand environmental variables. From an application and trust perspective, responsibilities should also be precisely defined. With sufficient attention to detail, we may be able to design and implement some useful applications for mobile devices.

8.2   Protecting Devices

The question of protecting devices often arises and should perhaps be further qualified by clarifying what we mean by device protection. Many will think of this as access control to the device in question or, more accurately, access to the operating system and applications which reside on the device. Biometrics may be perceived as a stronger method of user identity verification in this respect. However, we need to understand this in context. Mobile devices which offer biometric capability typically include a fallback position of a simple PIN (personal identification number) in order to cater for situations whereby the biometric identity verification has failed or for users who simply do not want to use such functionality. This practice effectively renders such devices as no more secure than any device which relies upon a simple PIN for access control. If more elaborate passwords are used, then the strength of the password will also have a bearing on both perceived and actual levels of security from an access control perspective. The same of course holds true for computer terminals and thin clients on networks. Consequently, the notion that a given device is somehow more secure because it features a biometrics is somewhat illusory. If access to a particular device is compromised by an individual who understands the device and its biometric capabilities, it may be that such an individual will temporarily enrol his or her own biometrics on the device, in order to enjoy any benefits associated with secondary identity verification via the biometrics. From the perspective of the receiving application, everything will be fine as the biometric identity check will have returned a positive result, even though the identity of the individual is not that to whom the device was registered. There may be additional checks that could be engineered into the device and its operating system, but there will always be a level of risk associated with access, just as there is, for example, with a user gaining root access to a computer on a network. There will always be a level beneath that of the biometric identity verification transaction, and this reality should be understood.

There is also the question of device protection from the perspective of attacks upon the device from an external source over a network, wireless or wired as the case may be. Any device which has access to an external network is vulnerable, to some degree or another. The 'out of the box' security settings of mobile devices and fixed clients will of course vary from one supplier to another. In the corporate world, where devices are supplied to employees for corporate use, a suitable security policy may be developed and applied to every device, further supported by suitable configured firewalls and other measures. For privately owned devices the situation is a little different. Some users will be diligent and will ensure that their device is configured to be as secure as is possible. Others will simply accept the standard settings, as supplied by the manufacturer. In recent times we have seen, unfortunately, that device suppliers cannot be trusted to implement a secure standard configuration. Indeed, certain suppliers have even taken the step of providing devices with preinstalled malware, deliberately designed to steal user-related information with the intent to pass this on to third parties for reasons of commercial gain. This may be a sad indictment of the modern world and the relationship between the supplier and consumer. It is also a matter of fact, which should be taken into consideration by users and prospective users of such devices. For mobile devices connected to a wireless network, there are all manner of risks involved as the device will be constantly exposed to malicious threats, including manipulation of the device itself by third parties. The salient point here is not to assume that the presence of biometric functionality somehow implies a higher level of security. From a transactional perspective, security, including device security, should be understood in relation to the end-to-end transaction and how the device in question functions throughout this transactional window, including device identity verification and user identity verification. Such factors will become increasingly important as mobile devices in particular will be used to verify payments. Naturally, there will be a wide variety of scams springing up in order to defraud both users and host applications. The implementation of biometric identity verification can add a valuable and additional level of confidence in this respect, providing that it is carefully orchestrated and that users are properly guided, including around areas of security overall.

8.3 Protecting Transactions

In addition to protecting devices, we need to consider how we protect transactions. The use of mobile devices for payments via wireless, near-field communications technologies is likely to mushroom and become pervasive across various retail, travel and other application sectors. Operators will have a higher confidence as to personal identity via a combination of mobile device identifiers and the use of biometrics in order to verify the identity of the user. It has been demonstrated that we cannot entertain absolute confidence as to the true identity of the user although, certainly, the biometric capabilities inherent in devices are likely to improve quite dramatically as the concept becomes embedded in everyday usage. However, as always, we must think of the end-to-end transaction and all the processes that are triggered along the way, together with protocols used and the relative security of our communications links. This latter point is particularly important at the initial interchange between the device and near-field reader. If it is possible to either interject or copy information as it traverses this link, then all manner of scams may be possible. From the near-field reading device onwards, we have a transaction of some kind and an intent of payment, perhaps via an interface with an acquirer or bank, and a final confirmation that the transaction is correct and has been completed. The data flow, from the client device through to back-end reconciliation and transaction completion, may pass through several stages and may reference one or more databases, each time acquiring or modifying information appertaining to the transaction at hand. Our confidence in the entire process may only be as strong as that of the performance and security of the weakest link. We therefore need to understand what that weakest link is (together with all the other less-weak links) and be able to quantify the level of risk accordingly. Factors such as end-to-end data encryption, device and user identity verification, secure interaction with acquirers and so on must all be considered in context. A good deal of the infrastructure shall, of course, already exist; however, we should not be complacent on this point as a new application provides us with an opportunity to revisit such areas and, if necessary, revise as applicable. In particular, we must strive to understand the interaction with the mobile device and the extent to which biometric identity verification has been successfully integrated. The assumption will be that, because a biometrics is present at all, this will infer a high level of security with respect to the device and its communications. This may or may not be realised in practice. We must understand what, exactly, the biometrics is doing. For example, do we understand where the matching threshold has been set? How exceptions are managed? What error rates may be under differing operational conditions? How easy or otherwise it might be to spoof the biometric? What provision has been made for users with disabilities? All these factors and more must be understood in relation to every such device on the market which might conceivably interact with the host application. Similar functionality for online transactions via fixed clients should also be considered. When designing such applications, the BANTAM methodology might prove useful as the various BANTAM maps and associated processes will help to inform discussion by allowing every step of the entire data flow to be documented and considered from a security perspective. Such an approach will also facilitate discussion and understanding between different entities involved in the end-to-end transactional chain. The use of the Biometrics Constitution and the Biometrics Charter Document will also prove invaluable in this context.

Much may be learned from current processes, especially where both low- and medium-value transactions occur. It may be that a good deal of the same infrastructure may be used, for example, the link with acquirers, although different policies may be in place for different types of transaction. Point-of-sale software will need to communicate with near-field devices, and this communications link must be properly understood, including aspects of performance and security. To this, we must add the interface with the client device and an understanding of what level of confidence we may entertain as to the true identity of the user. The whole concept represents an interesting development which will undoubtedly prove interesting to many. However, we must consider and understand the end-to-end transaction in its entirety, whatever that transaction is, from border crossing, to local benefits, to retail.

8.4   Privacy and Data Protection

Throughout our modern world we have more privacy and data protection acts and other legislative instruments than you can shake a stick at. These are supported, discussed and repeatedly chewed over by a veritable army of civil servants, consultants and so-called specialists. All of these directives, acts and other such mechanisms are, for most intents and purposes, completely meaningless as nobody, and especially the government agencies responsible for their creation, complies with them or shows any interest in enforcing them. They have become a parody of politically correct aspiration. The reality is that we have destroyed any notion of personal privacy and that personal data is anything but secure, being routinely shared, without either the explicit consent, or often even the knowledge of the user, between government agencies and with commercial interests the world over. Everybody steals and uses personal information for his or her own purposes and no one is ever brought to account. We never gave our permission for this; it is something that has been orchestrated by government and industry under the pretence of fighting organised crime, terrorism, money laundering, drug smuggling, human trafficking and other such emotive subjects. This surveillance regime has enabled law enforcement agencies to realise their dream of capturing the biometrics of almost the entire population, in the hope that they can simply match a sample from the scene of an incident, against what has become vast data sets of biometric and related information, and, indeed, in many cases this might be the case. However, in the process, they have effectively criminalised the innocent and made life miserable for ordinary, decent citizens, who are no longer differentiated from known criminals. Has it been worth the price? Has the world become a better or safer place? The answer to the latter question is an emphatic 'no'. Organised and violent crime continues to rise in our societies and many people no longer feel safe in their own neighbourhoods. Some will hold that the distinction between organised crime and government has also become blurred as ministers routinely engage in activities which, not so long ago, would have been considered unacceptable in any decent society. Indeed, anthropologists searching for an example of the criminal species often need look no further than their nearest government agency. Such is our twenty-first-century world.

One might ask what this has to do with biometrics and the design of related systems, especially as the current generation has been brought up in this environment of mistrust and often see nothing wrong with such practices. Does this mean that we should abandon any notion of privacy and data protection within our applications? No, it does not. Indeed, apart from the moral implications involved, there is good reason to go in the other direction and design in absolute privacy and protection for personal data. For many transactions, the identity of the user or consumer is actually unimportant. It is enough to know that they are eligible for a service or, in the context of a financial transaction, that the amount concerned will be paid. Many such transactions may therefore be undertaken anonymously, simply referencing a token or unique number which would only ever be linked back to the registered user in the event of a fraudulent transaction. In the latter instance, such referencing would only ever be undertaken by exception under strict guidelines, in response to clearly defined conditions and by named, qualified personnel. Furthermore, all such activity would be logged and subject to audit. The personal data involved would be encrypted, both in transit and at rest, and subject to the most stringent data security practices. This is all quite feasible and easily achieved within our contemporary technology framework. Within the context of a specific application, all data flows and communications protocols should be carefully considered from a data protection perspective. From an operational process perspective, our starting point should be that all transactions should be undertaken anonymously, unless there exists an exceptionally good reason why this cannot be the case. We may then design the system in a suitably secure manner and with full respect to personal privacy. It is curious that, for credit card transactions, we have the Payment Card Industry Data Security Standard (PCI DSS) that merchants are required to comply with. This has not been emplaced for the benefit of users but for the benefit of banks who want to minimise the risk of fraud. Nevertheless, it represents a useful step in encouraging merchants to consider data security and configure their systems and technical infrastructures accordingly. We could usefully adopt a similar approach with respect to the use of biometrics within broader applications. We have the Biometrics Constitution and the Biometrics Charter Documents as useful starters from the operational perspective and the BANTAM methodology for design purposes. This could be complemented by technical recommendations in a similar vein to the DSS but with explicit reference to biometrics.

In any event, there are many good reasons to take privacy and data protection seriously with regard to systems employing biometric identity verification. First of all, such a practice would be welcomed by users, especially if, via the Biometrics Charter Document, the application is properly described in terms of data flows and operational process, providing clarity as to exactly how the biometrics is being used and in what context. Such an approach would set a precedent for ethical systems design and those following it would attract a positive response from users. However, such an approach would also be a good policy with respect to both the security and the maintainability of the application overall. With everything intelligently designed and properly documented, the application becomes considerably easier to maintain with less risk of either inadvertent or malicious breaches of data. This makes good business sense as such an application will require less attention and, consequently, will be less expensive to maintain over the course of its natural span of operation. Such an approach would seem obvious, and yet, one might be surprised at how seldom it is followed in practice. One reason for this is a lack of proper ownership and management within the implementing agency. Indeed, the concept of ownership and responsibility has become considerably weaker in recent times, thus impacting both the operational efficacy and reliability of in-place systems. Technology is only part of the broader perspective. Operational process and robust management are equally important, although this fact seems to have been forgotten, especially by those agencies with a penchant to outsource everything to third parties. This culture of outsourcing and absolved responsibility has a direct relationship with privacy and data security. If we wish to take the concept seriously, we need to foster a much stronger hands-on approach with an emphasis upon ownership and responsibility. Such an approach, coupled with the use of the tools and mechanisms previously mentioned, will render positive results with respect to application security, privacy, ongoing maintenance and, indeed, operational cost. This is where our future aspirations should lay, especially with regard to the use of biometric identity verification.

8.5   Third-Party Environments

One of the most significant developments in information technology in recent years has been the emergence of the use of third-party environments, popularly known as the 'cloud'. It remains a wonder that so many have embraced this concept without really understanding its significance, especially from a data security perspective. The argument that such a practice cuts costs is, for most users, quite a ridiculous one as they already have their own environment and yet will pay extra just to be in the cloud. Furthermore, such costs are ongoing, from here to eternity, and will only ever rise. The reality is that those pursuing such a model will have absolutely no idea where their data is residing, upon what hardware and infrastructure and, importantly, who has access to that infrastructure and for what reason. Their operational data is effectively outside of their own control, residing, very often, in a completely different country and subject to whatever legislation, or lack of legislation, is in force at that locale. Unintelligent in the extreme, and yet, everyone seems to be rushing down this road, encouraged by the baying of the leading technology suppliers, all of whom stand to make substantial fortunes from the gullibility of the agencies and enterprises who seem incapable of thinking for themselves. We may forget any assurances from the technology suppliers as to the security or privacy of such data, as such proclamations are completely meaningless once the data has leaked from the host agency. Some will argue that there are some circumstances, such as when additional processing resource is required upon a temporary basis, where the use of such infrastructures makes sense. But even this is, at best, an extremely tenuous argument as one could easily, and inexpensively, maintain an in-house environment expressly for such occurrences. As users rely increasingly upon such third-party infrastructures, the availability of servers and hardware to private industry will become restricted and prices will rise, making it harder to get back to a properly controlled autonomous position wherein one is in full control of one's own data resources. Future historians will look back and wonder at the stupidity of both government and industry who so eagerly embrace any technological nonsense that is laid before them, each time paying more to do so.

In such environments the question of identity management quickly comes to the fore. If your organisation and, possibly, its effective 'customers' require access to this data, how is such access to be provided in a secure and ethical manner, and by whom? Will the third-party supplier maintain a directory of users, and, if so, how will this be secured and maintained? Will there be a separate directory for each consumer or will a single directory contain groups for such purposes? Who will manage this? How is this managed across virtual machines? There is an interest in what many describe as federated identity and the reuse of identity credentials across applications and infrastructures and, of course, no shortage of suppliers who claim to offer such a service. Exactly how federated identity would be securely managed is a factor often conspicuous by its absence, at least, in any sort of detail. Many suppliers propose using existing social network identities which are, of course, completely unauthenticated. The fact is that properly managing identity across disparate infrastructures, when you have no idea where those infrastructures actually are or who is administering them, represents a significant challenge. Assuming that the third-party infrastructure supplier may be relied upon to undertake this task while maintaining proper levels of privacy and data security would be an unrealistic and unqualified assumption, no matter how much technical propaganda is produced. Overlaying biometric identity verification onto such a model becomes especially interesting. First of all, who would be responsible for the registration process, and to what level of security would this be undertaken? If the infrastructure supplier is in a different country, as will often be the case, then this alone will be a significant issue. Assuming that the consumer organisation assumes responsibility for registering the biometrics, we still have the question of where the biometrics are stored and how they are used in relation to an identity verification transaction. If biometrics are stored in a directory residing upon the third-party infrastructure, then might one assume that that is also where the matching algorithm is stored and where the matching transaction will be undertaken. If that is the case, then the user's live biometrics will have to traverse all the network links from the client machine on the consumer organisation's premises to the back-end third-party infrastructure. How will the biometrics be sent? As an image in a standard image format? That would be especially insecure and open to data fraud. If the biometric image is encrypted, then to what standard, and what does this entail at both ends of the chain? Certainly, there would be performance implications. An alternative approach would be to manage the biometric identity verification at the client machine and simply send a pass/fail result over the network, together with some other unique identifiers. However, this would be open to spoofing and would negate the value of using a biometrics in the first place. Even if one were to find a workable solution architecturally, the problem of equivalence of performance across operational nodes would remain, with infrastructure suppliers adopting a matching threshold level completely autonomously. Depending upon the directory architecture being employed, it may well be possible to return more than one potential match, depending upon the identity verification methodology. The issue here is that, with matching threshold manipulation, it may be possible to provide a biometric identity verification model that gives the appearance of working tolerably well and, yet, is actually very weak with high probabilities of false positives which, of course, will not be recorded by the system.

There are all manner of possible variations, none of which would seem ideal when using third-party infrastructures. One approach may be to keep the biometric capability entirely within the control of the consuming organisation and use a successful match to release a token (such as a certificate) which may more easily be managed between the client and the hosted third-party infrastructure or service.

Properly designed, this may work well enough and would at least align the individual with the certificate rather than just the client machine. However, even with this model, there remain a number of issues to resolve. Nevertheless, we are sure to see an increasing interest in the use of biometrics for identity verification across third-party infrastructures, just as we shall see an increasing use of biometrics on mobile devices for payment purposes. In both cases, there is much to understand about the particular technical architecture being used and the associated implications for security. The fact that a biometrics is involved does not necessarily infer a higher level of security. Much depends upon precisely how the system has been designed, what matching methodology has been employed and what information is released upon the occurrence of a biometric match. In addition, and for each application, we must understand exactly what a biometric match is actually telling us. In all cases, it will be telling us that two examples of electronic data have been considered sufficiently alike to be considered as matching, according to a particular matching threshold and that, as a result, another data item (such as a 'passed' flag) is released into the data flow of the application. This is all that such a methodology can tell us. We still have the broader data flow to consider as well as the risks and benefits associated with a particular application. All of this becomes a little more obscured by the use of third-party environments and infrastructures. We need to understand this point if we choose to embrace such a model.

8.6   Operational Considerations

It is easy to consider the technology in isolation, discussing theoretical merits, issues and matters of performance, but technology does not exist in a vacuum. It is quite useless in itself and only becomes of value when applied to a particular situation, usually in the form of an application running on hardware of one sort or another. With a few exceptions, even the application is of no value until it receives input in the way of information, usually derived from real-world occurrences which, in turn, are often the result of human activity or interaction. This latter condition we encapsulate within the term 'process'. The situation in its entirety is thus a combination of technology and operational process, intermingled with human activity. Consequently, we must consider the operational process very carefully and ensure that the technology does not inhibit or limit the natural process. Unfortunately, it very often does just that and we have to find a compromise position which allows the technology to function in some sort of alignment with what may be termed the natural process. Biometric identity verification falls very much within this category. Our application will be more successful if we understand this juxtaposition between technology and process and cater for it accordingly.

The first step in the process is enrolment, the practice of registering one or more biometrics against a described identity. This first step often proves to be the weak link as, in many cases, the registration process is so weak and poorly managed that it is pitifully easy to create a fraudulent identity by registering a biometrics against false identity information. Consequently, there are an unknown number of passports, for example, which have been fraudulently registered and will likely never be discovered. This is the organised criminal's dream and one which has been readily facilitated by government, ensuring that many of the criminally inclined maintain multiple identities and multiple passports, all readily authenticated by a biometric check. This is one of the first things to understand about biometrics. The often stated notion that a biometrics proves you are who you say you are is completely false. It does nothing of the kind. A biometrics simply aligns an individual with an identity record which may or may not be accurate. The fact that a biometric check produces a positive match is neither here nor there. It does not prove or disprove an identity. In their haste to enrol as many citizens as possible in biometric databases, government agencies have unwittingly and undoubtedly created a swathe of fraudulent identities, each one of which may now be authenticated by a biometric check, often within an automated unmanned process. The criminals must have thought it was their birthday when such schemes were announced. The registration process is therefore absolutely vital and should be undertaken with the utmost care, checking and double-checking any documentary evidence that is provided and then cross-checking again by intelligent interview and, where necessary, verification by third parties. Government agencies will argue that they haven't the resources or time to introduce such an operational vigour, and yet, without this vigour, biometric identity verification becomes almost meaningless. Similarly with biometrics on mobile devices, if users are able to register their own biometrics, then, apart from personal use of the device, any external biometric check using such a reference is also rendered relatively meaningless. The irony is that, after more than 20 years of modern-day operations, many still cling to the belief that a biometrics proves identity. It does not. Whether the identity aligned with a biometrics is accurate or otherwise will depend very much upon the quality of the original registration process.

Assuming a good-quality registration process, the resulting identity record must then be protected from that point onwards. That entails data encryption, both at rest and in transit, coupled with a strong and auditable access control methodology, in place across all systems and subsystems where the biometric identity verification might take place. Furthermore, everything should be logged. Every transaction at every point of presence and every instance of access to an individual data record should be logged, with the logs themselves encrypted and stored for a minimum period, allowing independent audit by a trusted authority when necessary. How often is such a rigour applied to applications featuring this technology? If supplied by third parties, the answer will be hardly ever at all. Such an attitude of security and data protection must be designed in to the entire end-to-end process by the implementing agency itself. In the commercial world, it will make good sense to follow this approach in order to obviate against unnecessary errors and potential fraud.

The necessity to properly manage matching thresholds has been discussed and will be reiterated here, as it is a key factor from an operational perspective. If conventional fixed thresholds are used, then, across a medium- or large-scale system, the potential for operational disparity across nodes is very real and will generally increase over time as local operators attempt to fine-tune individual nodes. The use of a centralised control system, such as that described by the APEX methodology, will get around this problem by ensuring an equivalence of realised performance across operational nodes, although very few systems are so equipped. The use of the Proximity Matching Method would also provide substantially improved accuracy with fewer errors, regardless of the biometric technique chosen. The combination of both methodologies would represent a significant improvement in performance over the majority of in-place systems operating today. It will be interesting to see whether implementing agencies understand the relevance of this point and adopt a better approach to biometric sample matching as a result. Currently, there is considerable scope for improvement with most in-place systems. The same may be true of portable systems used, for example, in the military domain, often for quite different purposes. For those interested in user-managed biometrics on mobile devices, there are some quite obvious improvements that could be introduced to this particular model. Suffice it to say that, from an operational perspective, and in many cases, we could do better with regard to the efficacy of matching a live biometrics against a stored reference.

As previously mentioned, within the context of a system employing biometric identity verification, the user effectively becomes a systems component. It makes sense therefore to ensure that this 'user' component is properly understood, both in itself and with regard to how it interacts with other systems components. Many in-place applications, some of them of quite a high profile, are notoriously poor in this respect, with very little thought expended on users and how they interact with the system. In particular, the handling of exceptions is ill considered in many of these applications, often with an inherent attitude towards blaming the user if a transaction fails, believing that it must somehow be their fault and not that of the system. Such an attitude, oversimplistic and unintelligent as it is, seems to prevail within the context of a great many in-place systems. One would hope that such matters would have been learned by now, but apparently this is seldom the case when it comes to applications in the public domain. The use of the freely available tools and mechanisms described within this book would go a long way to improving this particular situation.

As an integral part of operational thinking and process design, we must of course understand the reason for implementing this technology in the first place, together with the associated benefits and risks, ensuring that the biometric check is actually performing a useful and meaningful function. This may not necessarily always be the case, especially if there is little understanding of what the results from a biometric matching transaction are actually telling us. If such usage may be properly justified, then the factors outlined in this chapter deserve very close attention in order to ensure that a suitable design statement be drawn up as a starting point, before rushing to implement a system as part of a politically correct initiative. For the majority of implementing agencies, there remains a great deal to understand around the practice of undertaking a biometric match and understanding what this really means in the context of identity verification. Similarly, there is much to understand from an end-to-end systems perspective, including the consideration of the user as an effective systems component. If one uses the Biometrics Constitution and the Biometrics Charter Document as intended, then the design, implementation and subsequent operation of the resulting application are likely to be better founded and therefore produce better results. It is time for a 'new deal for biometrics' whereby we introduce a new era of intelligent and thoughtful systems design, coupled to respect for users and full attention to matters of privacy and data protection. Actually, this is easily achieved if we have the will to do so.

8.7   Overall Conclusions

This second edition of *Practical Biometrics* has brought the original text up to date with developments in both the operational and technical world, ensuring its continued relevance to the practice of designing and implementing systems which incorporate biometric identity verification techniques. However, since the time of the first edition, much has changed in our world and we have witnessed a proliferation of applications and systems employing biometric technology. The bulk of these, in terms of physical presence and numbers of users, is connected with border control and law enforcement. In this context, a plethora of systems have been rolled out, largely based upon the assumption that a biometrics is proof of identity. The publicly declared rationale is that this is a necessary development in the fight against organised crime and terrorism. However, if we question whether our world has been made a safer or better place as a result of these initiatives, the answer is a resounding no; in fact, organised crime and instances of terrorism seem to have increased, to the point that no one feels safe anymore. This is a social development that can only be construed as negative, and, ironically, it is partly enabled by a worrying lack of control around economic and political migration, in spite of all the draconian identity checking taking place at airports. In addition, the almost paranoiac identity checking now taking place across the course of many transactions in public environments has resulted in a complete loss of privacy for ordinary citizens. Many feel that this is unjust and represents a backward step in civilisation overall, especially as it would appear to the layman that such measures have had little or no effect upon organised crime and terrorism. Furthermore, it makes one wonder about what life will be like for future generations if we persist in this attitude of mistrust and exploitation of ordinary, decent people, under the guise of fighting crime. Where is all this leading? Certainly not to a better society. Indeed, this general increase in surveillance of ordinary citizens has led to an increasingly oppressive society, fuelled by technology of all kinds, but especially information technology. If we continue along this path, the cost, in terms of quality of life and the damage to civilisation in general, will far outweigh any benefits associated with control. It is time that we started to take this situation seriously and re-examine both our intentions and our current practices.

There are of course practical benefits that may be realised by the application of biometric technology, provided that we keep things in perspective and resist the temptation to implement the technology wherever we can, simply because it is possible to do so. For example, in military situations especially, it is reasonable that, when issuing identity cards, one might include a biometrics in order to add a layer of confidence that the card is being presented by the individual to whom it was originally issued. Similarly, if this was all we did with passports, most people would not object. However, in many such applications there is no reason why the use of a biometrics should not be anonymous. It is simply not necessary to know *who* the individual is, as long as we have confidence that it is the *right* individual. The paranoia around law enforcement and the drive to collect the biometrics of the whole population are misplaced in this context as it does more harm to society than good. Furthermore, it is particularly disingenuous in that it fails to grasp what is perhaps the most important point, and that is the factor of intent. With all the surveillance in the world, it remains impossible to prejudge intent. An individual may have a change of attitude which leads them down a completely unexpected path, for better or worse. If it causes them to commit a crime, particularly a violent crime, then the fact that their records exist within a thousand and one databases will not deter them, as we see every day on our newsreels. While it is true that good intelligence on behalf of the agencies concerned may lead to the thwarting of criminal activities, the oppressive surveillance of ordinary, decent citizens has little to do with good intelligence. The focus should be upon those with serious criminal records where the probability of reoffending is high. Criminalising the innocent (which is exactly what has happened in recent years) does not help anyone, least of all the law enforcement and intelligence agencies whose job it is to protect society. It must be said that, in many countries, they are not making too good a job of it, in spite of a wealth of technology. Why mention this in a book which is ostensibly about the practical implementation of technology? Simply to emphasise that the implementation of technology for its own sake is meaningless. It only adopts a meaning when it is aligned with a societal situation. We must assure that such an alignment is positive and in the interest of the common good. Unfortunately, with respect to biometric technology, the alignment has become distorted as a result of political agendas which cannot be held to be in the common good. We must strive to ensure that we do not continue blindly along the current trajectory, but that we, instead, revaluate the situation completely and use our intelligence to apply such technologies only where it is genuinely useful to do so, from the broader societal perspective. We all have a responsibility in this respect, from government policy setters, through systems designers and technology suppliers, to those implementing agencies and other organisations who seek to deploy such technologies. Furthermore, this responsibility is not simply to ourselves and our peers but to future generations who will be raised within the society that we create and who will perpetuate the ideologies and methodologies that we provide.

This book has provided many ideas around the practical implementation of biometric identity verification technology. It has highlighted areas where mistakes are often made, as well as inherent weaknesses in both the technology and, especially, our assumptions around the technology. It has additionally offered a wealth of good advice, from a technical and operational perspective which, if followed, will undoubtedly lead to more successful implementations of the associated technologies. However, all of this is only part of the story. We must learn to think beyond the technology. We must develop a stronger understanding of how the systems that we put in place affect society. We must understand user psychology, not merely from an operational perspective (although this, in itself, is particularly valid) but from the broader societal perspective. Similarly, with respect to our intelligence services, we must beware of falling into the trap of over-reliance upon technology. Technology is a double-edged sword. It promises easier operation while robbing us of intellectual reasoning. It is important therefore to learn how to maintain a correct balance, between using technology where it really makes sense to do so, but not assuming that technology can replace human experience and intelligence. This is particularly relevant to the use of biometric technology, where so many (largely incorrect) assumptions are made about its efficacy in everyday use. As stated previously, technology itself is meaningless. It is the process to which we apply it that imbues it with meaning, and such processes must be intelligently considered and the resulting systems intelligently conceived. Consequently, the biggest advance we can make now is not with the technology itself but with our own understanding of how best to implement it in an intelligent and societally sympathetic manner. In addition, we ought to have a great deal more uniformity and equivalence of both process and realised performance than is currently the case. It is in pursuit of this latter objective that instruments such as the Biometrics Constitution and the Biometrics Charter Document have been developed, together with the BANTAM modelling methodology. Similarly, concepts such as the Proximity Matching Method and the APEX system of equivalence promote such aims. More recently, another initiative was proposed, expressly to bring a more unified approach to the process of border control. This was the InfoStrata concept, as covered in a popular technology journal read by many in this area. It outlined a complete methodology which, if adopted, would bring consistency and significantly improved performance to disparate applications. A good deal of work was expended upon this idea and an open invitation made for agencies to collaborate and develop it further. Unfortunately, no one came forwards to do so. This is mentioned in order to highlight the reality that politics plays in the implementation of such systems. We must find ways around this and encourage people to take a broader perspective. To date, and for precisely the same reasons, several high-profile systems are failing completely in their stated objectives. It is time for a different approach. Perhaps this book will offer some food for thought in this respect and encourage a new generation of technologists to think more seriously about the practical application of biometric technology. We can achieve much, with the right attitude and intelligent deliberation, but we need to guard against incorrect assumptions and we need a much firmer grasp on both technological and operational issues.

Readers will find a wealth of useful information, background papers and utilities, including all the software referred to in this book, on the Biometrics Research website, from where the author may also be contacted directly. The address is http://biometrics.bl.ee. Those who wish to comment, or possibly collaborate on the initiatives mentioned in this work, may also contact the author via the Biometrics Research website.

Index

Printed in the United States
By Bookmasters

Printed in the United States
By Bookmasters